Mongoose for Application Development

Learn to speed up your application development by using Mongoose to harness the power of Node.js and MongoDB

Simon Holmes

BIRMINGHAM - MUMBAI

Mongoose for Application Development

First published: August 2013

Production Reference: 1200813

Published by Packt Publishing Ltd.
Livery Place
35 Livery Street
Birmingham B3 2PB, UK.

ISBN 978-1-78216-819-5

www.packtpub.com

Cover Image by Abhishek Pandey (abhishek.pandey1210@gmail.com)

Credits

Author
Simon Holmes

Reviewers
Alexandru Vlăduțu

Robert Klep

David Harvey

Acquisition Editor
Grant Mizen

Commisioning Editor
Llewellyn Rozario

Technical Editor
Akashdeep Kundu

Project Coordinator
Joel Goveya

Proofreader
Mario Cecere

Indexer
Hemangini Bari

Production Coordinator
Aditi Gajjar

Cover Work
Aditi Gajjar

About the Author

Simon Holmes started his journey as a web developer in late 1990s. He built his first website for a project at university and soon saw what the industry had to offer when he promptly sold it! Following university, Simon worked his way through the ranks of design agency life, learning the skills of becoming a full-stack web developer. From server management and database design to building dynamic, UIs from Photoshop files, it all fell under Simon's remit. Having witnessed first-hand the terrible JavaScript code so prevalent in the early 2000s Simon is very much enjoying its resurgence as a powerful, structured language. Simon now works in SaaS, which is very heavy on the JavaScript.

Firstly I would like to thank my wife Sally for taking increased duties with our two lovely young daughters Eri and Bel, affording me some peace and quiet in which to code and write. Thanks also to Andreas Soellner for his feedback and encouragement throughout the process, and technical reviewers David Harvey of Vyclone Inc., Robert Klep, and Alexandru Vlăduțu. I also wish to express my thanks to the team at Packt Publishing who have been open and helpful from start to finish. Not forgetting of course Aaron Heckman who created Mongoose and continues to maintain, support, and push it forward.

About the Reviewers

David Harvey has built tools for more than twenty five years for developers, architectural infrastructure for investment banks, and high-end music software. He has formed and led teams in organizations of all sizes, and has taught, consulted, and presented on object technology, patterns and agile software development. He is currently the CTO at Vyclone Inc., delivering ground-breaking multi-angle video technology on mobile and cloud platforms.

Robert Klep is a freelance frontend and backend web developer from 's-Hertogenbosch, the Netherlands, with more than 17 years experience. Lately, Robert has been focusing more on JavaScript and Node.js development. He has used Mongoose extensively in several projects. He was the winner of the 0th Annual Obfuscated Perl Contest in 1996.

Alexandru Vlăduțu is a JavaScript developer at a company in Bucharest, Romania. He started creating applications with PHP five years ago, but after finding out about server-side JavaScript with Node.js he never had to switch technologies again. You may have seen him answering questions on stackoverflow.com under the nickname alessioalex, where he is in the top three overall answerers for tags like Node.js, Express, Mongoose, or Socket.IO. By day he battles cross browser compatibility issues, but by night he brings together embedded databases, servers, and caching layers into single applications using the good parts of JavaScript. Aside from the geeky stuff, he enjoys spending time with his wife.

I would like to thank the Node.js community for being so friendly and helpful.

Most importantly, I would like to thank my wife Diana for her support, encouragement, and patience.

www.PacktPub.com

Support files, eBooks, discount offers and more

You might want to visit www.PacktPub.com for support files and downloads related to your book.

Did you know that Packt offers eBook versions of every book published, with PDF and ePub files available? You can upgrade to the eBook version at www.PacktPub.com and as a print book customer, you are entitled to a discount on the eBook copy. Get in touch with us at service@packtpub.com for more details.

At www.PacktPub.com, you can also read a collection of free technical articles, sign up for a range of free newsletters and receive exclusive discounts and offers on Packt books and eBooks.

http://PacktLib.PacktPub.com

Do you need instant solutions to your IT questions? PacktLib is Packt's online digital book library. Here, you can access, read and search across Packt's entire library of books.

Why Subscribe?

- Fully searchable across every book published by Packt
- Copy and paste, print and bookmark content
- On demand and accessible via web browser

Free Access for Packt account holders

If you have an account with Packt at www.PacktPub.com, you can use this to access PacktLib today and view nine entirely free books. Simply use your login credentials for immediate access.

Table of Contents

Preface

Mongoose for Application Development will show you how to leverage the power of Mongoose to dramatically speed up your development process with Node.js and MongoDB. At the highest level, Mongoose is all about having a data model, and bringing control and management of that model into your application. Mongoose enables you to create a robust yet rich data structure, providing you with a level of database management that you don't normally get with MongoDB. With its built-in helper methods, Mongoose provides a lot of the common functionality you will need, while also providing a framework for extending it in ways to meet your application needs.

What this book covers

Chapter 1, Introducing Mongoose to the Technology Stack, takes a look at the Node.js, MongoDB, and Express technology stack and introduces Mongoose and shows where it fits in.

Chapter 2, Establishing a Database Connection, covers the different methods of creating database connections with Mongoose, including how and when to use them.

Chapter 3, Schemas and Models, introduces the two cornerstones of Mongoose, covering how to create them and how they relate to the data.

Chapter 4, Interacting with Data – An Introduction, explains how Mongoose provides methods for easily interacting with data, setting the scene for the following four chapters.

Chapter 5, Interacting with Data – Creation, covers the ways we can use Mongoose to create data and save it to the database.

Chapter 6, Interacting with Data – Reading, Querying, and Finding, covers the ways we can use Mongoose to find the data we want by querying the database and reading the data back into Model instances. It shows how to use the built-in methods, and also how to extend Mongoose to run the specific queries that you may want.

Chapter 7, Interacting with Data – Updating, covers the ways we can use Mongoose to change existing data, including the built-in helper methods, and a more robust approach for data integrity.

Chapter 8, Interacting with Data – Deleting, covers the ways we can use Mongoose to delete documents from the database.

Chapter 9, Validating Data, looks at maintaining data integrity, covering the validators built in to Mongoose and explaining how to add custom validation.

Chapter 10, Complex Schemas, introduces the concepts of population and sub-documents to allow richer data models, mimicking some of the functionality found with traditional SQL JOIN statements.

Chapter 11, Plugins – Reusing Code, introduces the Mongoose plugin architecture, covering how to create your own re-usable plugins to remove repetition in your schemas.

What you need for this book

All you need for this book is a computer capable of running Node.js, administrator/installation permissions, and a text editor.

Who this book is for

This book is for people who are interested in building applications in Node.js. If you want to build applications quickly with a robust and manageable data structure then this book is for you! No experience with Node is necessary, but some basic knowledge of HTML and JavaScript would be useful. The focus of the book is on the power of Mongoose, so experienced Node.js developers will also find it useful.

Conventions

In this book, you will find a number of styles of text that distinguish between different kinds of information. Here are some examples of these styles, and an explanation of their meaning.

Code words in text, database table names, folder names, filenames, file extensions, pathnames, dummy URLs, user input, and Twitter handles are shown as follows: "You may find that your installation of Express has already created the file `routes/user.js` — this is fine, you can just open it and delete the contents."

A block of code is set as follows:

```
var userSchema = new mongoose.Schema({
   name: String,
   email: {type: String, unique:true},
   createdOn: Date,
   modifiedOn: { type: Date, default: Date.now },
   lastLogin: Date
```

When we wish to draw your attention to a particular part of a code block, the relevant lines or items are set in bold:

```
var express = require('express')
 , db = require('./model/db')
 , routes = require('./routes')
 , user = require('./routes/user')
 , project = require('./routes/project')
```

Any command-line input or output is written as follows:

```
$ sudo apt-get install npm
```

New terms and **important words** are shown in bold. Words that you see on the screen, in menus or dialog boxes for example, appear in the text like this: "If it finds it, MongoDB (not Mongoose) will return an **E11000** error.".

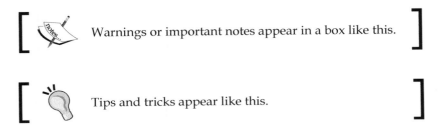

[Warnings or important notes appear in a box like this.]

[Tips and tricks appear like this.]

Reader feedback

Feedback from our readers is always welcome. Let us know what you think about this book—what you liked or may have disliked. Reader feedback is important for us to develop titles that you really get the most out of.

To send us general feedback, simply send an e-mail to feedback@packtpub.com, and mention the book title via the subject of your message.

If there is a topic that you have expertise in and you are interested in either writing or contributing to a book, see our author guide on www.packtpub.com/authors.

Customer support

Now that you are the proud owner of a Packt book, we have a number of things to help you to get the most from your purchase.

Downloading the example code

You can download the example code files for all Packt books you have purchased from your account at http://www.packtpub.com. If you purchased this book elsewhere, you can visit http://www.packtpub.com/support and register to have the files e-mailed directly to you.

Errata

Although we have taken every care to ensure the accuracy of our content, mistakes do happen. If you find a mistake in one of our books—maybe a mistake in the text or the code—we would be grateful if you would report this to us. By doing so, you can save other readers from frustration and help us improve subsequent versions of this book. If you find any errata, please report them by visiting http://www.packtpub.com/submit-errata, selecting your book, clicking on the **errata submission form** link, and entering the details of your errata. Once your errata are verified, your submission will be accepted and the errata will be uploaded on our website, or added to any list of existing errata, under the Errata section of that title. Any existing errata can be viewed by selecting your title from http://www.packtpub.com/support.

Piracy

Piracy of copyright material on the Internet is an ongoing problem across all media. At Packt, we take the protection of our copyright and licenses very seriously. If you come across any illegal copies of our works, in any form, on the Internet, please provide us with the location address or website name immediately so that we can pursue a remedy.

Please contact us at copyright@packtpub.com with a link to the suspected pirated material.

We appreciate your help in protecting our authors, and our ability to bring you valuable content.

Questions

You can contact us at questions@packtpub.com if you are having a problem with any aspect of the book, and we will do our best to address it.

1

Introducing Mongoose to the Technology Stack

We are going to take a look at the technology stack we'll be using throughout the book. After a brief discussion of Node, npm, MongoDB, and Express we will introduce Mongoose as an **ODM (Object-Document Modeler)**, cover good and bad use cases, and introduce the two cornerstones of Mongoose.

By the end of this chapter you will have an understanding of the technology stack and where Mongoose fits in. We will also have set up the sample project that we will build throughout the book.

The technology stack – Node.js, npm, MongoDB, and Express

The benefits of Node are making it ever more popular, and a set of compatible technologies are fast becoming the basis of a new standard development stack.

The language and the server – JavaScript and Node

For quite some time JavaScript was mainly thought of as a lightweight browser-based scripting language. Microsoft did support a JavaScript version of Classic ASP, but it was largely side-lined in favor of the VBScript version.

Fast-forward 10 years and there were some pretty impressive JavaScript-based apps on the Web, for example Gmail. The general view of JavaScript as a programming language was starting to change back then.

In 2010 a new server-side system called **Node.js** was starting to make waves in the Internet developer community. Node.js was a new way for using JavaScript on the server side again. And it was quick and efficient. It could make scaling a web application much more cost-effective by reducing the amount of hardware required per-site visitor or request.

By 2012 Node was one of the buzzwords of the start-up scene, and you can see why. Firstly, most Web developers have some JavaScript experience so it doesn't require you to learn a new language from scratch. This also means you can share some code between front-end and back-end, so you don't have to code the same thing twice in two different languages. An excellent example of this is form validation; you want real-time validation in the browser for a better user experience, but you also need to validate on the server side to protect your system. So you code the same thing twice. Using Node you can use the same validation script on the server side and the browser, so you only have to code it once, in JavaScript.

Second, there is the reduced cost of scaling, especially when dealing with large numbers of concurrent users. On the same hardware Node's efficiencies allow it to handle many more requests than classic stacks on Apache or IIS. That being said, adding scalability to Node is more complicated than other stacks. Unlike the others you can't just put it on a more powerful machine and set it running. By default Node will currently only run one process, using only one core of a machine. There are methods to address this issue, using a load balancer in front of several processes running alongside each other for example, and there are plans to enable future versions of Node to be able to manage this natively, directly addressing this issue.

The benefits of scalability do have a cost. The single process is a more complicated approach to server-side programming and requires a change in mindset.

Single-threaded versus multithreaded

Traditional stacks are generally **multithreaded**. This means that every new visitor or session is given a new thread, and these are never shared. One session's activity generally doesn't impact another, until the server resources are exhausted. For example, if `Session 1` is doing a complex database write operation it may take a couple of seconds, but `Session 2` continues running oblivious to this.

Node is **single-threaded**. This means that every visitor or session is added to that one thread. So it is possible for a two-second database write operation to hold up every other user for two seconds. Multiply this by just 10 users and you've got a big problem on your hands.

Addressing this requires a different way of coding.

Blocking versus non-blocking code

In the traditional stack, the approach to coding would be one step after the other, as in the following steps:

1. First, take the data.
2. Then write this data to the database.
3. Send a confirmation message.
4. Wait for the next request.

This is **blocking** code, as you can only do one thing at a time. This is fine in the multithreaded stack, as you're only ever responding to one person's requests.

In the single-threaded stack, you may have to respond to several people's requests at the same time, so you can't afford to be stuck doing time-consuming operations or waiting for someone else to do something. To do this, the approach to coding becomes more like the following:

1. You give this data to someone.
2. They write this data to the database.
3. When they are done, they send a confirmation message; if this isn't something they can do, then they add it to your request list.
4. You're going to take the next request.

This is **non-blocking** code. You can only do one at a time. So you're getting someone else to do something for you, and telling them what to do when they have finished. You can then deal with the next request coming in without any delay.

JavaScript callbacks

The way to code this in JavaScript is to use callbacks. Most JavaScript coders start using them before they even know it, particularly anybody who uses libraries such as jQuery.

Take the basic jQuery document.ready method as shown in the following:

```
$(document).ready(function() {
  console.log("document ready");
});
```

This is an event driven callback. The $(document).ready() part is a method function of jQuery, and we are sending it a function function() that it can run at the appropriate time. So we are saying "Hi ready, here is what I want you to do once the document is ready, I'll leave it up to you to decide when that is". The callback function we are using in this example is the following code snippet:

```
function() {
  console.log("document ready");
}
```

Running the callback

The jQuery .ready() function is pretty complicated, so we're not going to look at that here. However, the construct is very useful to understand. Look at the following code snippet:

```
ready = function (callback) {
  // do something
  // do something else
  // ....
  // and so on
  callback();
};
```

So ready itself is a function, and this function accepts one parameter callback. The callback parameter is generally an anonymous function, like the one we looked at earlier. A very important point to note is that callback now exists in the scope of the ready function. This means that your callback function has access to any variables or objects created in the ready function.

A Node.js example

Now consider the following standard Node "hello world" example:

```
var http = require('http');
http.createServer(function (req, res) {
  res.writeHead(200, {
    'Content-Type': 'text/plain'
  });
  res.write('Hello world');
res.end();
})
listen(8888, '127.0.0.1');
```

Look familiar? This is sending a callback to the `http.createServer` method function. See how the parameters — `req` and `res` — are being sent to the callback function even though they haven't been defined or created anywhere. This works because the `http.createServer` function will create these objects before calling this callback function that will use them.

The database – MongoDB

MongoDB has become the main database of choice for working with Node. Note that there are Node drivers for many other databases, including MySQL, Microsoft SQL Server, Reddis, PostgreSQL, CouchDB, and more.

MongoDB is popular as it is fast and flexible with excellent community support. It is a document-oriented database, fitting in somewhere between Key-Value stores and traditional relational databases. Despite being a document store, MongoDB also enables rich querying and secondary indexing of documents, setting it apart from other databases and making it a very powerful option.

MongoDB stores documents as BSON, which is effectively binary-encoded JSON. When you run a query you get a JSON object returned (or a string in JSON format, depending on the driver). Look at the following code snippet for example:

```
{ "_id" : ObjectId("4ffbc45c35097b5a1583ad71"),
  "firstname" : "Simon", "lastname" : "Holmes" }
```

So, a document is a set of keys (for example, `firstname`) and values (for example, `Simon`). The `_id` entry is a unique identifier that the underlying MongoDB driver will — by default — create for each new document.

If you are more experienced with relational databases, it may help you to think of a document as a bit like a row in a table. In this analogy, the **key** can be thought of as a column. An important difference is that each document doesn't have to contain the exact same set of keys, and there is no direct need to have keys with empty values taking up space.

A collection of documents is called a **collection**. The closest analogy is a table. So in your database you could well have multiple collections, such as a users collection, posts collection, and stats collection.

MongoDB is also extremely scalable, with many built-in capabilities for distributing across multiple servers, without compromising speed or data integrity.

With everything combined, it makes MongoDB a great playmate for Node.

The framework – Express

Express is a web application framework for Node.

When you create a Node project, you have to do a lot more groundwork than you might be used to. Until you create it, there isn't even a web server. Then you have to deal with serving static files in a non-blocking way, figure out the routing mechanism, view engine, session management, and so on.

Or you can create an Express project and let it do all of this for you, in a tried-and-tested way. At the end of this chapter, we'll see how easy it is to set up an Express project.

Note that Express is not required to build a Node application, but it is a great starting point for building web applications.

What Mongoose is all about

Mongoose is an object modeling tool for MongoDB and Node.js. What this means in practical terms is that you can define your data model in just one place, in your code.

Yes, that's right. You don't have to create a schema in the database, link that to an ORM or map it into your project objects and classes. You can just define your data structure in JSON inside your project.

The first time I created a project like this I was amazed at how much time and frustration it saves. Even now I still get that warm glow when I start a new project or prototype using Mongoose. It's like taking a shortcut to work down deserted country lanes while everybody else is gridlocked on the highway.

A schema definition can be as simple as the following code snippet:

```
var userSchema = new mongoose.Schema({
  firstname: String,
  lastname: String,
  createdOn: Date
});
```

A document in MongoDB created from this schema would be like the following code snippet:

```
{ "__v" : 0, "_id" : ObjectId("51412597e8e6d3e35c000001"),
  "createdOn" : ISODate("2013-03-14T01:19:19.866Z"),
  "firstname" : "Simon", " lastname " : "Holmes" }
```

If you want to refactor, then you can just do it from within your code, saving a huge amount of development time.

What is Mongoose good for?

Mongoose is primarily useful when you want to interact with structured data in MongoDB. It allows you to define a schema for your data, so that you can interact with your MongoDB data in a structured and repeatable way.

Mongoose helps with many common MongoDB tasks, and removes some of levels of complexity from the nested callbacks you find yourself getting lost in with the native MongoDB driver.

Mongoose also returns the data to you as a JSON object that you can use directly, rather than the JSON string returned by MongoDB.

Mongoose also has a whole suite of helper functions and methods that we'll explore throughout the subsequent chapters of this book.

What Mongoose is not ideally suited for

Mongoose is probably not the answer for you if you are primarily working with the following:

- Schema-less data
- Random documents
- Pure Key-Value pairs

The cornerstones of Mongoose

There are two aspects of Mongoose that we need to introduce you to before going much further:

- Schemas
- Models

This is a very high-level view; so don't worry if you're not 100 percent confident with this just yet, as we'll be covering it in a lot more detail later in this book.

Mongoose schemas

As we saw earlier, a **schema** is fundamentally describing the data construct of a document. This schema defines the name of each item of data, and the type of data, whether it is a string, number, date, Boolean, and so on.

```
var userSchema = new mongoose.Schema({
    name: String,
    email: String,
    createdOn: Date,
    verified: Boolean
});
```

In most scenarios you would have one schema for each collection within the database.

Schemas are a powerful aspect of Mongoose, which can also be extended with helper functions and additional methods. But we'll describe more about that in a later chapter.

Mongoose models

A **model** is a compiled version of the schema. One instance of the model will map to one document in the database.

Creating a User instance based on the schema userSchema is a one line task:

```
var User = mongoose.model('User', userSchema);
```

It is the model that handles the reading, creating, updating, and deleting of documents.

Installing the full stack

Now that we know a little bit about the technology, it's time to get everything installed. What follows is not an in-depth installation tutorial, but covers the necessary steps to get everything installed on Ubuntu. The installation process is very similar on other Linux distributions and Mac OS X. For Windows users, Node and MongoDB have installation packages you can run, and after that everything else is pretty much the same.

Installing the prerequisites

Node needs a couple of things installed to run properly, Python and a C compiler. So let's make sure those are installed and up-to-date with a terminal command. I use the Ubuntu **Advanced Packaging Tool** (**APT**) to install most software, as it makes it this easy:

```
$ sudo apt-get install python-software-properties python g++ make
```

Installing Node.js

Again we'll use APT to install Node.js. As Node is actively developed and frequently updated, APT doesn't always have the latest build. The latest version on APT is currently several versions behind, so we will add the repository of one of the Node.js developers. This is also the approach recommended on the Node website nodejs.org.

```
$ sudo add-apt-repository ppa:chris-lea/node.js
```

```
$ sudo apt-get update
```

```
$ sudo apt-get install nodejs
```

If everything has gone smoothly then you should be able to check the installed version displayed in terminal using the following command:

```
$ node --version
```

You should be greeted with a message back in the terminal along the lines of **v0.10.0**.

Installing npm

npm is a package manager for Node, although npm does not actually stand for Node Package Manager. As of Node Version 0.6.3, npm is actually automatically installed when you install Node.

You can quickly check that this has been done by checking the version number on the terminal.

```
$ npm --version
1.1.23
```

If it is not there for some reason, simply install it with APT with the following command:

```
$ sudo apt-get install npm
```

Installing MongoDB

Again we're using APT here.

```
$ sudo apt-get install mongodb
```

In order to test MongoDB, we need to run it. You can do this by just typing mongodb into terminal, but I prefer to run it as a persistent service so that you don't have to restart it.

```
$ sudo service mongodb start
```

This should give you a confirmation message in terminal that the mongodb process is running.

Now to finally test that it has installed correctly we'll drop into the built-in MongoDB shell. In terminal, enter the following:

```
$ mongo
```

This should do three things:

- Enter you into the MongoDB shell
- Show you the version of the shell being used
- Connect to the test database that comes with MongoDB

You should see something like the following screenshot:

Installing Express.js

Now we're starting to get into the Node-based applications. So those of you who are working on different operating systems can start paying attention again now. We are going to install Express using npm.

```
$ sudo npm install -g express
```

 See the -g flag there in the command line? This installs express globally, meaning that we can use it wherever we want.

Once again you can test the installation by checking the version number.

```
$ express --version
```

Installing Mongoose

Finally we get round to installing Mongoose!

There are two ways of installing Mongoose, both using npm. I recommend using the latter one.

Direct installation into project

If you're creating a quick test app, or will never have to move or publish the project elsewhere, you can use npm to install Mongoose directly into your project. Navigate to the root folder of your site or project in terminal and run the following command:

```
$ sudo npm install mongoose
```

Using project dependencies – package.json

Any Node project can have a `package.json` file, and any packages you install via npm will have one. This file is normally in the root of your project, and can contain various metadata, such as `project name`, `description`, `version number`, and `authors`. It also helps manage the project's dependencies.

If you ever need to move, copy, or distribute your project you will find this invaluable. The dependency management means that you are not forced to remember which versions of which modules you added to each particular project. It becomes even more necessary if you distribute it widely, as it removes any doubt from the end-user's mind as to what the project needed.

Before we get into creating one, the following code snippet is an example of a `package.json` file following code snippet that you might expect to see when you create a new project using Express.

```
{
  "name": "application-name",
  "version": "0.0.1",
  "private": true,
  "scripts": {
    "start": "node app"
  },
  "dependencies": {
  "express": "3.0.0rc5",
  "jade": "*"
  }
}
```

 The list of dependencies are: a specific version of express and the latest version of jade.

To install a specific version of Mongoose — which is the recommended approach, especially if you are going to distribute your project — you would update the dependencies section to look like the following code snippet:

```
"dependencies": {
  "express": "3.0.0rc5",
  "jade": "*",
  "mongoose": "3.6"
}
```

To install or update all of the dependencies listed in a `package.json` file, using terminal, you simply navigate to the folder containing the file and run the following command:

```
$ npm install
```

Creating a project

Now that we have the entire building blocks ready, let's set the foundations. Throughout this book, we are going to build a simple project management web app, called **MongoosePM**.

Let's start off by creating an Express project.

1. In terminal, navigate to a relevant folder, for example, /MyWebsites in Linux, or C:\Users\Your Username\Documents\My Web Sites\ in Windows.

2. Enter the following command:

```
$ express --sessions mongoosepm
```

This will create a new folder called mongoosepm. Inside this folder it will create a new Express project. By default an Express project doesn't support user sessions; an Express project is essentially stateless. By adding the --sessions parameter in the command line we add session support to our project, so that we can follow a user from page to page without having to constantly re-authenticate.

After Express has finished doing its thing you'll be able to see a whole load of new files and folders within your mongoosepm folder. The intricacies of Express are beyond the scope of this book, which is one of the reasons we have mainly stuck with the default settings.

The next step is normally to install the dependencies, but first let's add Mongoose and Connect to the dependency list. So open up the package.json file in the root of the project and add a couple of lines to the dependencies hash.

For example, if your dependencies section looks like the following code snippet:

```
"dependencies": {
  "express": "3.0.0rc5",
  "jade": "*"
}
```

Then you change it with this (see the following code):

```
"dependencies": {
  "express": "3.0.0rc5",
  "jade": "*",
  "connect": "2.7.x",
  "mongoose": "3.6.x"
}
```

It is recommended that you don't "wildcard" the version for most modules, as there is no guarantee that code based on older versions will work on newer versions. Putting a wildcard in for the patch version like we have for Connect and Mongoose, is recommended as they should only be patch updates and be backwards compatible.

To install these dependencies, go to the `mongoosepm` folder in terminal and run the following command:

```
$ npm install
```

Once this has finished working, we should have a fully functional Express website to play with. Let's test it to make sure!

Run the following command from terminal:

```
$ node app
```

You should see the following confirmation message directly in terminal:

Express server listening on port 3000

So open up a web browser, and point it to `http://localhost:3000`. All being well, you should be presented with the default Express project landing page, as shown in the following screenshot:

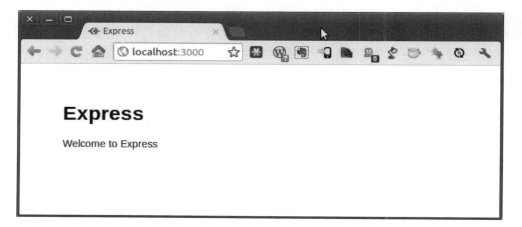

Downloading the example code

You can download the example code files for all Packt books you have purchased from your account at `http://www.PacktPub.com`. If you purchased this book elsewhere, you can visit `http://www.PacktPub.com/support` and register to have the files e-mailed directly to you.

Summary

In this chapter we have taken a whirlwind tour of the technology stack, and installed the required programs, which are as follows:

- Node.js
- npm
- MongoDB
- Express
- Mongoose

You should have at least a basic understanding of the majority of the stack. We're not going to be discussing in depth the workings of Node, MongoDB, and Express, but I will make sure to briefly describe any new concepts as we go.

In this first chapter, we have also created the framework for the project that we are going to build in later chapters. This is a website built on Node.js, using the Express framework. We have tested and seen this working in a browser.

In the next chapter, we will take a look at how to create Mongoose connections to database, and the best way to add a connection to our new project.

2
Establishing a Database Connection

We are going to look at the two methods Mongoose uses to connect to databases, `mongoose.connect` and `createConnection`. We will also go through various configuration options.

By the end of this chapter, you will understand how to best use the different Mongoose connection methods to meet your needs. We will also have added a connection to the MongoosePM example project.

Mongoose default connection

The way to set the default connection to a MongoDB database via Mongoose is nice and easy, using the `mongoose.connect` method.

```
var dbURI = 'mongodb://localhost/mydatabase';
mongoose.connect(dbURI);
```

This will open a Mongoose connection to the Mongo database `mydatabase`, running on the server `localhost`. If established at the correct place in your code, this connection will now be available at any point in your app, if you *require* Mongoose.

Best practice

The best practice for a default Mongoose database connection is to open it when the application starts, and keep it open to be re-used. The connection should only need to be closed if your app is being shut down or restarted.

Using multiple connections

The default connection is great if your app only needs to connect to one database. But what happens if you need to connect to a second database at the same time? Or connect to the same database as a different user with different permissions.

For this we can use the `mongoose.createConnection` method, which is as follows in the code snippet:

```
var dbURI = 'mongodb://localhost/myadmindatabase';
var adminConnection = mongoose.createConnection(dbURI);
```

About the connection string

The connection string—`dbURI` in our examples—can use any of the options from the MongoDB connection string. We're not going to cover them all here, but here are a couple of common options.

Setting the port

The default port is 27017. If you wanted to specify a different port, say 27018, you would do so using the following code snippet:

```
var dbURI = 'mongodb://localhost:27018/mydatabase';
```

Specifying a database user

If you want to access the database as a particular user, you can add the username and password in front of the hostname.

```
var dbURI = 'mongodb://username:password@localhost/mydatabase';
```

Connection options

Mongoose allows you to pass certain options through to both connection methods. If specified, these options will override those set in the connection string.

The options are sent as a JSON object as an optional second parameter to the connection call. For example:

```
var dbURI = 'mongodb://localhost/mydatabase';
var dbOptions = {'user':'db_username','pass':'db_password'};
mongoose.connect(dbURI, dbOptions);
```

The options you can use this way are:

- **user and pass**: Username and password for the database, if required and not specified in the connection string.

- **db**: This relates to the DB options available in the Node MongoDB Native driver.

- **server**: This relates to the server options available in the Node MongoDB Native driver.

- **replset**: This option allows you to specify a ReplicaSet. The details of ReplicaSet methods are beyond the scope of this book, but the principle is that you can have one primary database where all the writes are made to, and multiple secondary databases. If the primary database fails, one of the secondary databases is automatically made the new primary.

Closing the connection

As we have already seen, the general best practice is to open your connection at application start up, and keep it open. However, there are times when you will want to close the connection. For example, if your application is shutting down, or restarting, the database connection needs to be manually closed, or if you are running a single-hit script rather than a persistent application.

Calling the close command

Each Mongoose connection has a `close()` method that takes an optional callback function.

If you are using the default connection you call it like the following code snippet does:

```
mongoose.connection.close(function () {
  console.log('Mongoose default connection closed');
});
```

Calling the `close()` method on a named connection is just as easy, using our example from earlier:

```
adminConnection.close(function () {
  console.log('Mongoose connection adminConnection closed');
});
```

Closing when the Node process ends

As a rule you should tidy up the connections when your Node application stops, whether this is an intentional process termination or not. To do this, you can send your disconnections as a callback to Node's `process.on('SIGINT')` event as shown in the following:

```
process.on('SIGINT', function() {
  mongoose.connection.close(function () {
    console.log('Mongoose disconnected through app termination');
    process.exit(0);
  });
});
```

Connection events

The connection process in Mongoose inherits the Node `EventEmitter` class, meaning that we can set certain code to run following specific events. We can—and will—work with some of the connection events, such as `connected`, `disconnected`, and `error`.

The connection events are all used in the same way, sending a callback to the `connection.on` event listener. For example, if we wanted to log to the console when a connection error occurs we could do this in the following code:

```
mongoose.connection.on('error',function (err) {
  console.log('Mongoose connection error: ' + err);
});
```

Connecting our project

Now we know what we're doing, let's connect our project to a database using the default Mongoose connection.

Creating the connection

For the sake of well organized code, let's create a folder called `model`, and in that, an empty JavaScript file called `db.js`. We'll use this for managing the Mongoose connection, and will add to it in later chapters.

At this stage the file needs to do three things:

1. Bring in the Mongoose module

2. Build the connection string for the database

3. Open the Mongoose connection to the database

So in your /model/db.js file, enter the following:

```
// Bring Mongoose into the project
var mongoose = require( 'mongoose' );

// Build the connection string
var dbURI = 'mongodb://localhost/MongoosePM';

// Create the database connection
mongoose.connect(dbURI);
```

Each of the three objectives is achieved with just one line of code — pretty simple don't you think!

Catching the events

Next up we want to set up our event handlers. At this stage, we are just going to log messages to the console, but they are useful containers, and important to understand. We will also catch when the Node process is ending and close the Mongoose connection.

So, still in db.js, after the connection code add the following snippets:

```
mongoose.connection.on('connected', function () {
  console.log('Mongoose connected to ' + dbURI);
});

mongoose.connection.on('error',function (err) {
  console.log('Mongoose connection error: ' + err);
});

mongoose.connection.on('disconnected', function () {
  console.log('Mongoose disconnected');
});

process.on('SIGINT', function() {
  mongoose.connection.close(function () {
    console.log('Mongoose disconnected through app termination');
    process.exit(0);
  });
});
```

Opening the connection at application start

Now we need to tell the project to use this file, so that we can connect to the database when the application starts. This is as simple as requiring our new file in `app.js` — you may remember that this is the file we run to start the application.

At the top of your `app.js` file you should see some of the default modules being required like in the following:

```
var express = require('express')
  , routes = require('./routes')
```

We are simply going to add one line in here, to require our `model/db.js` file immediately after `express` is required. You should end up with something resembling this following code:

```
var express = require('express')
  , db = require('./model/db')
  , routes = require('./routes')
```

Creating the database

You will notice that we haven't actually created a MongoDB database yet. The good — and perhaps surprizing — news is that we don't have to. Nor do we have to explicitly create any collections.

MongoDB will create a database the first time anything is saved to it, and the same for collections.

I love this approach. This is one of the aspects that I find really speeds up application development and prototyping.

You can of course connect to an existing database, if you already have one.

Summary

In this chapter, we have looked at the two methods of creating a Mongoose connection to a MongoDB database, and when you would use each method.

We have learned that the best practice is to create a connection when your application starts and keep it open to be re-used. Tied to this we have seen how and when to close the connection, and how to act upon events emitted by the connection process.

We have also taken a brief look at how to specify different options if you have a more complex database setup, or want to override some defaults.

You should now have connected your MongoosePM project to the MongoosePM database, even though the database doesn't exist yet!

In the next chapter, we're going to start getting stuck into the real meat of Mongoose, by defining schemas and models.

Schemas and Models

3

We are going to look at the two building blocks of Mongoose, schemas, and models. We will look at their relationship to the data and how they can be used to maximize the effectiveness of Mongoose. This chapter covers fairly simple schemas; more complex schemas will be explored in *Chapter 10, Complex Schemas*.

By the end of this chapter, you will understand the roles of schemas and models and their relationship to the data. We will also add schemas and models to the MongoosePM example project.

Introducing schemas

So what is a schema? At its simplest, a **schema** is a way to describe the structure of data. Typically this involves giving each piece of data a label, and stating what type of data it is, for example, a number, date, string, and so on.

As we have already seen in *Chapter 1, Introducing Mongoose to the Technology Stack*, a schema definition in Mongoose is a JSON object. In the following example, we are creating a new Mongoose schema called userSchema. We are stating that a database document using this schema will have three pieces of data, which are as follows:

- name: This data will contain a string
- email: This will also contain a string value
- createdOn: This data will contain a date

The following is the schema definition:

```
var userSchema = new mongoose.Schema({
  name: String,
  email: String,
  createdOn: Date
});
```

Field sizes

Note that, unlike some other systems there is no need to set the field size. This can be useful if you need to change the amount of data stored in a particular object. For example, your system might impose a 16-character limit on usernames, so you set the size of the field to 16 characters. Later, you realize that you want to encrypt the usernames, but this will double the length of the data stored. If your database schema uses fixed field sizes, you will need to refactor it, which can take a long time on a large database. With Mongoose, you can just start encrypting that data object without worrying about it.

If you're storing large documents, you should bear in mind that MongoDB imposes a maximum document size of 16 MB. There are ways around even this limit, using the MongoDB GridFS API.

Data types allowed in schemas

There are eight types of data that can—by default—be set in a Mongoose schema. These are also referred to as SchemaTypes; they are:

- String
- Number
- Date
- Boolean
- Buffer
- ObjectId
- Mixed
- Array

The first four SchemaTypes are self-explanatory, but let's take a quick look at them all.

String

This SchemaType stores a string value, UTF-8 encoded.

Number

This SchemaType stores a number value, with restrictions. Mongoose does not natively support `long` and `double` datatypes for example, although MongoDB does. However, Mongoose can be extended using plugins to support these other types. See *Chapter 11, Plugins – Re-using Code* for more on plugins.

Date

This SchemaType holds a date and time object, typically returned from MongoDB as an ISODate object, for example, `ISODate("2013-04-03T12:56:26.009Z")`.

Boolean

This SchemaType has only two values: `true` or `false`.

Buffer

This SchemaType is primarily used for storing binary information, for example, images stored in MongoDB.

ObjectId

This SchemaType is used to assign a unique identifier to a key other than _id, for example, a foreign key for referencing another document (see *Chapter 10, Complex Schemas* for more about this). Rather than just specifying the type of `ObjectId` you need to specify the fully qualified version `Schema.Types.ObjectId`. For example:

```
projectSchema.add({
  owner: mongoose.Schema.Types.ObjectId
});
```

Mixed

A `mixed` data object can contain any type of data. It can be declared either by setting an empty object, or by using the fully qualified `Schema.Types.Mixed`. These following two commands will do the same thing:

```
vardjSchema= new mongoose.Schema({
  mixedUp: {}
});
vardjSchema= new mongoose.Schema({
  mixedUp: Schema.Types.Mixed
});
```

While this sounds like it might be great, there is a big caveat. Changes to data of `mixed` type cannot be automatically detected by Mongoose, so it doesn't know that it needs to save them.

Tracking changes to Mixed type

As Mongoose can't automatically see changes made to `mixed` type of data, you have to manually declare when the data has changed. Fortunately, Mongoose exposes a method called `markModified` to do just this, passing it the path of the data object that has changed.

```
dj.mixedUp = { valueone: "a new value" };
dj.markModified('mixedUp');
dj.save();
```

Array

The `array` datatype can be used in two ways. First, a simple array of values of the same data type, as shown in the following code snippet:

```
var userSchema = new mongoose.Schema({
  name: String,
  emailAddresses: [String]
});
```

Second, the array datatype can be used to store a collection of subdocuments using nested schemas. We'll explore this concept further in *Chapter 10, Complex Schemas*, but for now here's an example in the following of how this can work:

```
var emailSchema = new mongoose.Schema({
  email: String,
  verified: Boolean
});
var userSchema = new mongoose.Schema({
  name: String,
  emailAddresses: [emailSchema]
});
```

Warning – array defined as mixed type

A word of caution. If you declare an empty array it will be treated as `mixed` type, meaning that Mongoose will not be able to automatically detect any changes made to the data. So avoid these two types of array declaration, unless you intentionally want a `mixed` type.

```
var emailSchema = new mongoose.Schema({
  addresses: []
});
var emailSchema = new mongoose.Schema({
  addresses: Array
});
```

Custom SchemaTypes

If your data requires a different datatype which is not covered earlier in this chapter, Mongoose offers the option of extending it with custom SchemaTypes. The extension method is managed using Mongoose plugins, which we'll look at in detail in *Chapter 11, Plugins – Re-using Code*. Some examples of SchemaType extensions that have already been created are: `long`, `double`, `RegEx`, and even `email`.

Where to write the schemas

As your schemas sit on top of Mongoose, the only absolute is that they need to be defined after Mongoose is *required*. You don't need an active or open connection to define your schemas.

That being said it is advisable to make your connection early on, so that it is available as soon as possible, bearing in mind that remote database or replica sets may take longer to connect than your localhost development server.

While no action can be taken on the database through the schemas and models until the connection is open, Mongoose can buffer requests made from when the connection is defined. Mongoose models also rely on the connection being defined, so there's another reason to get the connection set up early in the code and then define the schemas and models.

Writing a schema

Let's write the schema for a User in our MongoosePM application.

The first thing we have to do is declare a variable to hold the schema. I recommend taking the object name (for example, `user` or `project`) and adding `Schema` to the end of it. This makes following the code later on super easy.

The second thing we need to do is create a new Mongoose schema object to assign to this variable. The skeleton of this is as follows:

```
var userSchema = new mongoose.Schema({ });
```

We can add in the basic values of `name`, `email`, and `createdOn` that we looked at earlier, giving us our first user schema definition.

```
var userSchema = new mongoose.Schema({
  name: String,
  email: String,
  createdOn: Date
});
```

Modifying an existing schema

Suppose we run the application with this for a while, and then decide that we want to record the last time each user logged on, and the last time their record was modified. No problem!

We don't have to refactor the database or take it offline while we upgrade the schema, we simply add a couple of entries to the Mongoose schema. If a key requested in the schema doesn't exist, neither Mongoose nor MongoDB will throw errors, Mongoose will just return null values. When saving the MongoDB documents, the new keys and values will be added and stored as required. If the value is null, then the key is not added.

So let's add `modifiedOn` and `lastLogin` to our `userSchema`:

```
var userSchema = new mongoose.Schema({
  name: String,
  email: String,
  createdOn: Date,
  modifiedOn: Date,
  lastLogin: Date
});
```

Setting a default value

Mongoose allows us to set a default value for a data key when the document is first created. Looking at our schema created earlier, a possible candidate for this is `createdOn`. When a user first signs up, we want the date and time to be set.

We could do this by adding a timestamp to the controller function when we create a user, or to make a point we can modify the schema to set a default value.

To do this, we need to change the information we are sending about the `createdOn` data object.

What we have currently is:

```
createdOn: Date
```

This is short for:

```
createdOn: { type: Date }
```

We can add another entry to this object to set a default value here, using the JavaScript `Date` object:

```
createdOn: { type: Date, default: Date.now }
```

Now every time a new user is created its `createdOn` value will be set to the current date and time.

Note that in JavaScript `default` is a reserved word. While the language allows reserved words to be used as keys, some IDEs and linters regard it as an error. If this causes issues for you or your environment, you can wrap it in quotes, like in the following code snippet:

```
createdOn: { type: Date, 'default': Date.now }
```

Only allowing unique entries

In *Chapter 9, Validating Data*, we will be looking at how we can use Mongoose to validate data, but here is a quick way to ensure that there are no duplicates for a specific data item.

For example, if we want to ensure that there is only ever one user per e-mail address, we can specify that the `email` field should be unique.

```
email: {type: String, unique:true}
```

With this in place, when saving to the database, MongoDB will check to see if the e-mail value already exists in another document. If it finds it, MongoDB (not Mongoose) will return an **E11000** error. Note that this approach also defines a MongoDB index on the `email` field.

We'll look at more validation techniques in *Chapter 9, Validating Data*.

Our final User schema

Your `userSchema` should now look like the following:

```
var userSchema = new mongoose.Schema({
  name: String,
  email: {type: String, unique:true},
  createdOn: { type: Date, default: Date.now },
  modifiedOn: Date,
  lastLogin: Date
});
```

A corresponding document from the database would look like the following (line breaks are added for readability):

```
{ "__v" : 0,
"_id" : ObjectId("5126b7a1f8a44d1e32000001"),
"createdOn" : ISODate("2013-02-22T00:11:13.436Z"),
"email" : "simon@theholmesoffice.com",
"lastLogin" : ISODate("2013-04-03T12:54:42.734Z"),
"modifiedOn" : ISODate("2013-04-03T12:56:26.009Z"),
"name" : "Simon Holmes" }
```

What's that "__v" thing?

You may have noticed a data entity in the document that we didn't set: __v. This is an internal versioning number automatically set by Mongoose when a document is created. It doesn't increment when a document is changed, but instead is automatically incremented whenever an array within the document is updated in such a way that might cause the indexed position of some of the entries to have changed.

Why is this needed?

When working with an array you will typically access the individual elements through their positional index, for example, `myArray[3]`. But what happens if somebody else deletes the element in `myArray[2]` while you are editing the data in `myArray[3]`? Your original data is now contained in `myArray[2]` but you don't know this, so you quite happily overwrite whatever data is now stored in `myArray[3]`. The __v gives you a method to be able to sanity check this, and prevent this scenario from happening.

Defining the Project schema

As part of our MongoosePM application we also need to think about Projects. After all, PM here does stand for Project Manager.

Let's take what we've learned and create the Project schema. We are going to want a few types of data to start with:

- `projectName`: A string containing the name of the project.
- `createdOn`: The date when the document was first created and saved. This option is set to automatically save the current date and time..
- `modifiedOn`: The date and time when the document was last changed.
- `createdBy`: A string that will for now contain the unique ID of the user who created the project.
- `tasks`: A string to hold task information.

Transforming these requirements into a Mongoose schema definition, we create this in the following:

```
varprojectSchema = new mongoose.Schema({
  projectName: String,
  createdOn: Date,
  modifiedOn: { type: Date, default: Date.now },
  createdBy: String,
  tasks: String
});
```

This is our starting point, and we will build upon it when we look at more complex schemas in *Chapter 10, Complex Schemas*. For now we have these basic data objects as mentioned previously in this chapter.

Here's an example of a corresponding document from the database (line breaks added for readability):

```
{ "projectName" : "Another test",
"createdBy" : "5126b7a1f8a44d1e32000001",
"createdOn" : ISODate("2013-04-03T17:47:51.031Z"),
"tasks" : "Just a simple task",
"_id" : ObjectId("515c6b47596acf8e35000001"),
"modifiedOn" : ISODate("2013-04-03T17:47:51.032Z"),
"__v" : 0 }
```

Improving the Project schema

Throughout the rest of the book we will be improving this schema, but the beauty of using Mongoose is that we can do this relatively easily. Putting together a basic schema like this to build upon is a great approach for prototyping—you have the data you need there, and can add complexity where you need, when you need it.

Building models

If you remember from *Chapter 1, Introducing Mongoose to the Technology Stack*, a model is a compiled version of the schema.

A single instance of a model maps directly to a single document in the database. With this 1:1 relationship, it is the model that handles all document interaction—creating, reading, saving, and deleting.

This makes the model a very powerful tool.

Building the model, as we have seen, is pretty straightforward. When using the default Mongoose connection we can call the `mongoose.model` command, passing it two arguments:

- The name of the model
- The name of the schema to compile

So if we were to build a model from our user schema we would use this line:

```
mongoose.model( 'User', userSchema );
```

If using a named Mongoose connection, the approach is very similar. Using the `adminConnection` example from *Chapter 2, Establishing a Database Connection*:

```
adminConnection.model( 'User', userSchema );
```

Instances

We'll be looking at how we interact with the data in the next chapter, but it is useful to have a good understanding of how a model works.

After building the `User` model, using the previous line we could create two instances.

```
var userOne = new User({ name: 'Simon' });
var userTwo = new User({ name: 'Sally' });
```

Interacting with instances

Each instance is a JavaScript object that we can interact with.

```
console.log(userOne.name); // 'Simon'
userOne.name = 'Simon Holmes';
console.log(userOne.name); // 'Simon Holmes'
```

As each new `User` is an instance of the model, we are able to use the power of the model to save it to the database as shown in the following code:

```
userTwo.save(function (err) {
  if (err) return handleError(err);
  // userTwo (Sally) is saved!
});
userOne.save(function (err) {
  if (err) return handleError(err);
  // userOne (Simon Holmes) is saved!
});
```

Finding a single instance

If we ask Mongoose to "find one", we expect a single instance to be returned. This looks like the following code snippet:

```
User.findOne({'name' : 'Sally', function(err,user) {
if(!err){
  console.log(user);
  }
});
```

The output of this `console.log` is a single instance:

```
{
  name: 'Sally',
  _id: 515c6b47596acf8e35000001,
  __v: 0
}
```

Finding many instances

If we use a "find many" command, we expect to get an array of instances:

```
User.find({}, function(err, users) {
  if(!err){
    console.log(users);
  }
});
```

The output of this `console.log` is an array of instances:

```
[ {
  name: 'Sally',
  _id: 515c6b47596acf8e35000001,
  __v: 0 },
{
  name: 'Simon Holmes',
  _id: 515c6b47596acf8e35000002,
  __v: 0
} ]
```

Considerations when choosing your model name

Unless specified, the MongoDB collection will be a pluralized (lowercase) version of the model name. See the following for example:

```
mongoose.model( 'User', userSchema );
```

The previous line will reference a collection called `users`. If the collection doesn't exist it will create it the first time a document is saved using the model.

 The collection name defaults to a pluralization of the Mongoose model name.

Setting the collection name

Having a default collection name is great when you're creating an application from scratch, but what if you're using an existing database with collection names that don't match this approach?

There are two ways of specifying a different collection name

- Using either the schema declaration, or
- The model command

Overriding the collection name in the schema

To specify a collection name when defining a schema you need to send a second argument to the `new mongoose.Schema` call.

Say we have an existing collection called `myuserlist` that we want to use with our `userSchema`, the following snippet is how we would do it:

```
var userSchema = new mongoose.Schema({
  name: String,
  email: {
    type: String, unique:true
  }
},
{
  collection: 'myuserlist'
});
```

Overriding the collection name in the model

To specify the collection name when building a model you send a third argument to the `mongoose.model` command.

Using the same example as before, here's how it looks when setting the collection name through the model command:

```
mongoose.model( 'User', userSchema, 'myuserlist' );
```

Building models from our schemas

Now let's put the theory into action, and build the models from our User and Project schemas.

In the `/model/db.js` file, add the following after the `userSchema` is defined:

```
// Build the User model
mongoose.model( 'User', userSchema );
```

And add the following after the `projectSchema` is defined:

```
// Build the Project model
mongoose.model( 'Project', projectSchema );
```

This will give us everything we need to start interacting with data in our application, which we will start doing very soon, in the next chapter.

Our complete code

Now that we have defined our schemas and compiled the models, let's take a look at our /model/db.js file.

```javascript
var mongoose = require( 'mongoose' ),
dbURI = 'mongodb://localhost/MongoosePM';
mongoose.connect(dbURI);
// Connection events snipped out for brevity


/* *********************************************
      USER SCHEMA
   ********************************************* */
var userSchema = new mongoose.Schema({
  name: String,
  email: {type: String, unique:true},
  createdOn: { type: Date, default: Date.now },
  modifiedOn: Date,
  lastLogin: Date
});

// Build the User model
mongoose.model( 'User', userSchema );

/* *********************************************
      PROJECT SCHEMA
   ********************************************* */
var projectSchema = new mongoose.Schema({
  projectName: String,
  createdOn: { type: Date, default: Date.now },
  modifiedOn: Date,
  createdBy: String,
  contributors: String,
  tasks: String
});

// Build the Project model
mongoose.model( 'Project', projectSchema );
```

In this code we have done everything we need to before moving on. These are as follows:

- We *required* Mongoose
- We set the connection string for the MongoDB database

- We defined the User schema
- We built the User model
- We defined the Project schema
- We built the Project model
- We opened the Mongoose connection to the database

Note that if you have large complex schemas and models, you may want to have separate files for each, and just export the models.

Summary

In this chapter, we have looked at how schemas and models relate to your data. You should now understand the roles of both schemas and models.

We have looked at how to create simple schemas and the types of data they can contain. We have also seen that it is possible to extend this if the native types are not enough. On top of this we have learned about compiling the schemas into models and had a glimpse at how powerful this set of tools can be.

In the MongoosePM project, you should now have added a User schema and a Project schema, and built models of both of these.

In the next chapter, we're going to see how we use these schemas and models to create, read, update, and delete data.

4

Interacting with Data – an Introduction

We have seen how to define our data structure, but now we want to interact with it. We want to be able to create database entries, read them, update them, and delete them. To handle these interactions, Mongoose uses methods added to models. This chapter introduces the concept and will look at how to organize our code to best work with this approach.

By the end of this chapter, you will have had a glimpse of how Mongoose helps you to easily interact with your data. You will also have prepared the sample project so that we can dive into practical examples in later chapters.

Model methods and instance methods

As we have seen in *Chapter 3*, *Schemas and Models*, a document in a Mongoose collection is a single instance of a model. So it makes sense that if we're going to work with our data then it will be through the model.

So what do we mean by model methods? Well, if we have a model called `User`, some of the methods provided by Mongoose are `User.create`, `User.find`, `User.update`, and `User.remove`. The method names may be slightly different, but out of the box we've got methods for all four CRUD (Create, Read, Update, and Delete) operations right there.

Instance methods are the same concept, except that they are applied to specific instances instead. We will look at a good example of this soon, with the `instance.save` method.

Mongoose also allows you to define your own model methods, giving you the flexibility to create the functionality you want. We'll see more about these static methods and create one ourselves in *Chapter 6, Interacting with Data – Reading, Querying, and Finding*.

Before we look at some examples, first let's remind ourselves of our `User` schema and model so that we can use this as the basis.

```
var userSchema = new mongoose.Schema({
  name: String,
  email: {type: String, unique:true},
  createdOn: Date,
  modifiedOn: { type: Date, default: Date.now },
  lastLogin: Date
});


// Build the User model
mongoose.model( 'User', userSchema );
```

So we have our model called `User`, compiled from the schema `userSchema`. Got it? Good. Now let's get our project ready so that we can use the examples as we go!

Setting up the project

Before we get going on the Mongoose code, we need to get a couple of things in order in our project:

- Our approach to code structure
- The URLs/routes we'll need

Code structure

If we think in an MVC way, our Express project already has a model folder and a views folder. The model folder holds our schema definitions, Mongoose models and Mongoose connection. The views folder contains Jade templates for page layout. The controller aspect sits in the routes folder of a standard express installation. We could separate it out or move it around, but as the focus of this book is on using Mongoose, but not on MVC best practices, let's work with the default setup.

Adding the routes files

A good starting point when thinking about setting up your routes is to have one routes file for each Mongoose model. Given the non-normalized data structure of MongoDB there aren't generally too many of these—we're not talking about individual tables in a relational database here! Also, as we saw earlier in this chapter, we are generally working with model methods, and instances of that model. So it seems like a sensible way to separate out our code in the first instance.

So with that in mind, create two empty text files in the routes folder, user.js and project.js. You may find that your installation of Express has already created the file routes/user.js—this is fine, you can just open it and delete the contents.

Bear in mind that as your applications grow in complexity, these files can get very large, in this case you may want to divide them in a logical way for your application.

Tying the routes to Mongoose models

In each of these files, we need to require Mongoose and the relevant model. So at the top of the user.js file add the following:

```
var mongoose = require( 'mongoose' );
var User = mongoose.model( 'User' );
```

And add the following to project.js:

```
var mongoose = require( 'mongoose' );
var Project = mongoose.model( 'Project' );
```

We need to get these files into the application, so we'll require them in app.js. You'll see that routes is already required, and we'll keep that to hold our index page. Let's add our two new files user and project directly after it.

```
var express = require('express')
  , db = require('./model/db')
  , routes = require('./routes')
  , user = require('./routes/user')
  , project = require('./routes/project')
```

URLs and routes

Next up we need to think about how we're going to interact with the data and the URLs we're going to use to do it. These will all go into app.js immediately after the homepage route.

Routes for user management

We will concentrate on the user management first, so we will want to have the following:

- User homepage or profile page at /user
- Login page at /login
- New user form at /user/new
- Edit current user details form at /user/edit
- Delete user confirmation form at /user/delete
- Logout user action at /logout

In most of these options, we want a form and an action to do something, so we will use both app.get for displaying forms and app.post for form handling. So let's add these routes in to app.js below the following app.get('/', routes.index) in app.js, defining our route function names as we go. See the following code snippet:

```
app.get('/', routes.index);
// USER ROUTES
app.get('/user', user.index);              // Current user profile
app.get('/user/new', user.create);         // Create new user form
app.post('/user/new', user.doCreate);      // Create new user action
app.get('/user/edit', user.edit);          // Edit current user form
app.post('/user/edit', user.doEdit);       // Edit current user action
app.get('/user/delete', user.confirmDelete); // delete current
                                           //user form
app.post('/user/delete', user.doDelete);   // Delete current
                                           //user action
app.get('/login', user.login);            // Login form
app.post('/login', user.doLogin);          // Login action
app.get('/logout', user.doLogout);         // Logout current user
```

Routes for project management

We are going to take a similar approach for dealing with projects, except that project information won't be stored in a session. So to tell a page which project we are working with, we will include the unique ID in the URL. Add the following code to app.js below the user routes that we have just added:

```
// PROJECT ROUTES
app.get('/project/new', project.create);      // Create new
                                              //project form
app.post('/project/new', project.doCreate);   // Create new
                                              //project action
```

```
app.get('/project/:id', project.displayInfo); // Display project
                                    //info
app.get('/project/edit/:id', project.edit);   // Edit selected
                                    //project form
app.post('/project/edit/:id', project.doEdit);// Edit selected
                                    //project action
app.get('/project/delete/:id', project.confirmDelete);// Delete
                                    // selected product form
app.post('/project/delete/:id', project.doDelete);    // Delete
                                    //selected project action
```

Summary

In this chapter, we have had a very quick glance at how Mongoose provides methods for us to interact with our data. We have also seen how to set up our project to work with Mongoose, attaching our schemas and models to the actual back end of the application.

In the next four chapters, we will be exploring the Mongoose data methods in much greater detail, focusing around the cornerstones of CRUD operations. First up, *Chapter 5, Interacting with Data – Creation*, for creating data.

5
Interacting with Data – Creation

As we are building an application from the ground up, our first work with data will be creating some and saving it to the database. In this chapter we will:

- Learn about creating an instance
- Learn about saving an instance
- Learn when to use different approaches
- Add the ability for users to sign up to our MongoosePM application by:
    ◦ Adding new routes
    ◦ Adding new views
    ◦ Adding new controller code
    ◦ Saving the user details in a session so that they stay logged in

- Outline the steps required to add the ability to create new projects, but let you go for it alone! If you get stuck, you can always download the complete source code to take a look.

Creating an instance

Now that *Chapter 4, Interacting with Data – An Introduction* has taken care of the housekeeping, it's time to get going and do stuff with data. Theory first, then action!

To do anything meaningful at all, we will have to create an instance. This could be done by retrieving an object from a database, but let's start by creating a new empty instance. We do this by using the `new ModelName` expression. As our model is called `User`, to create a new instance we invoke the `new User` expression.

```
var newUser = new User();
```

Adding data to the instance

When creating an instance, you will generally want to add some data to it. The default way of adding data is to pass it to the model constructor as a JavaScript object. For example:

```
var newUser = new User({
  name: 'Simon Holmes',
  email: 'simon@theholmesoffice.com',
  lastLogin : Date.now()
});
```

Although you can also add data to the instance after it has been created, as shown in the following:

```
var newUser = new User();
newUser.name = 'Simon Holmes';
```

Or you can use a combination, setting some data when the object is created, and adding additional data afterwards:

```
var newUser = new User({
  email: 'simon@theholmesoffice.com',
  lastLogin : Date.now()
});
newUser.name = 'Simon Holmes';
```

Saving an instance

So far we have created an instance, and put some data to it, but it only exists in the application. Saving it to the database is a really simple operation.

 Your Mongoose connection must be open for this to work.

After we have created our `newUser` and given it some data, we save it in the following way:

```
newUser.save( function( err ){
  if(!err){
    console.log('User saved!');
  }
});
```

This `.save` method is an example of an instance method, because it operates directly on the instance, rather than the model. Note that the parameter it takes is a callback function to run when the save operation has been made to the database. As we saw back in *Chapter 1, Introducing Mongoose to the Technology Stack*, writing to a database is a blocking operation, but the `.save` method provides a non-blocking asynchronous way of doing this, allowing the Node process to carry on and deal with other requests.

This is a good thing for our application, but it means that any operations that you want to do *after* the instance is saved must come *inside* the callback function.

 Any default values set in the schema are automatically applied when `.save` is called, before the data is saved to the database.

Using the saved data

The `.save` method allows you to specify a second parameter to the callback, which will contain the saved object. Your callback function can then use this object. This can be useful in many ways, for example, if you want to find out the unique ID of the database entry you have just created. The code to do that looks like this:

```
newUser.save( function( err, user ){
  if(!err){
    console.log('Saved user name: ' + user.name);
    console.log('_id of saved user: ' + user._id);
  }
});
```

Here we are returning the saved user information in the `user` object, which would look like the following lines (line breaks added for readability):

```
{ "__v" : 0,
"_id" : ObjectId("5126b7a1f8a44d1e32000001"),
"createdOn" : ISODate("2013-02-22T00:11:13.436Z"),
```

```
"email" : "simon@theholmesoffice.com",
"lastLogin" : ISODate("2013-04-03T12:54:42.734Z"),
"modifiedOn" : ISODate("2013-04-03T12:56:26.009Z"),
"name" : "Simon Holmes" }
```

In our callback function, we can use any of this data using standard dot syntax. In the case of this example code we've gone for `user.name` and `user._id`.

`_id` is an `ObjectId` SchemaType (see *Chapter 3, Schemas and Models*) that is unique and automatically added by Mongoose. You can also access a string representation of it by removing the underscore. This means we could also have the following:

```
console.log('id of saved user: ' + user.id);
```

This can cause confusion when comparing the two, as while these may look the same when sent to the console, one is an `ObjectId` and the other is a string.

Creating and saving database entry in one step

We don't always need to run all the commands separately and can simplify do things by creating and saving the database entry in one step. There are two ways of doing this.

Chaining methods

The first way is to chain the `newUser` and `.save` commands into one line, for example:

```
var newUser = new User({
  name: 'Simon Holmes',
  email: 'simon@theholmesoffice.com',
  lastLogin : Date.now()
}).save( function( err ){
  if(!err){
    console.log('User saved!');
  }
});
```

The Model.create() method

The second way is to use a single-model method, which combines the `new` and the `save` operations into one command. This method takes two parameters. First is the data object, and the second is the callback function that is to be executed after the instance has been saved to the database.

So the blueprint for this method is:

```
ModelName.create(dataObject,callback)
```

Let's see this in operation, using our trusty `User` model:

```
User.create({
  name: 'Simon Holmes',
  email: 'simon@theholmesoffice.com',
  lastLogin : Date.now()
}, function( err, user ){
  if(!err){
    console.log('User saved!');
    console.log('Saved user name: ' + user.name);
    console.log('_id of saved user: ' + user._id);
  }
});
```

This is arguably the neater way of doing a brand new create and save operation, and is the approach we'll be using in our MongoosePM application later. The cost of the compact nature of this approach is that it is less flexible, as we can't do anything with the `newUser` instance between creating it and saving it. If you need this flexibility, then go for the `new` and `save` approach, like in the following:

```
var newUser = new User({name: 'Simon Holmes'})
newUser.email = 'simon@theholmesoffice.com';
var rightNow = Date.now();
newUser.createdOn = rightNow;
newUser.lastLogin = rightNow;
          // some more operations on newUser
newUser.save( function( err, user ){
  if(!err){
    console.log('_id of saved user: ' + user._id);
  }
});
```

CRUD – create data

Now we're going to take what we've just learned, and use it to add the ability to create users in our application. If we look back to the routes we set up in `app.js`, we can see that we have two routes for creating a user, the form itself and the form action.

```
app.get('/user/new', user.create);        // Create new user form
app.post('/user/new', user.doCreate);      // Create new user action
```

Adding a new user form

To display the form in an HTML page, we need to do two things:

- Create the Jade template
- Link the template to the route

Adding the Jade template

By default Express will install with two Jade template files, `layout.jade` and `index.jade`. The layout template contains the HTML skeleton, including the DTD, `<head>`, and `<body>` tags. The index template extends the layout template inside the `<body>` tag.

For our MongoosePM application, we will keep this simple approach, and create a new extension template for each new page template we need. This is a great approach for rapid prototyping and development of a proof of concept. But before releasing an app, you'll probably want to spend more time on the templates and layout.

Let's get started and create the template file for our user sign-up form. In the views folder either copy `index.jade` or create a blank text file and call it `user-form.jade`. In that file, enter the following lines and save it:

```
extends layout

block content
  h1= title
  form(id="frmUserProfile", method="post", action="")
    label(for="FullName") Full name
    input(type="text", name="FullName", id="FullName")
    label(for="Email") Email
    input(type="email", name="Email", id="Email")
    input(type="submit", value="#{buttonText}")
```

Here you can see that we are extending the template `layout`, and defining a block of code for the `content` section of the layout template.

For the rest of the templates in this book, we will omit the `extends layout` and `block content` lines for brevity, unless they are required to set context.

This page is going to be pretty minimal, having a `<h1>` tag containing the page title that we'll pass through as the variable title, and a blank form. The form only asks for the full name and e-mail address; the submit button expects a variable `buttonText` to be passed to the template and will use it for the `value`. We have set the form method to POST and left action blank. This means that the form will post to the same URL that is displaying the form. If we look back at our routes this is the behavior we are looking for:

```
app.get('/user/new', user.create);      // Create new user form
app.post('/user/new', user.doCreate);   // Create new user action
```

This is a technique we'll be using a few more times in this application.

Linking the view to the URL

Now that we have our display template ready, we need to link it to the routing. Our routing maps a GET request of the URL /user/new to the route user.create. So in our /routes/user.js file we need to create an export function called create. As part of this, we need to send the variables that the Jade template is expecting: title and buttonText. Your function should look something like the following:

```
// GET user creation form
exports.create = function(req, res){
  res.render('user-form', {
    title: 'Create user',
    buttonText: "Join!"
  });
};
```

That's pretty straightforward right? We can easily see this in action by running our application.

Restarting the application

If your application is still running, then refreshing the page in the browser will not reflect changes made to Node.js code, although you will generally see changes made to Jade and CSS files. To restart the application, go to the terminal window running the process and hit *Ctrl + C* to kill the process. Then run the following command ensuring that you are in the root folder of the application:

```
$ node app
```

Alternatively there are a few tools available to monitor and restart your Node server automatically, such as **Nodemon** and **Supervisor**, which are available at the following links:

```
https://github.com/remy/nodemon
```

and

```
https://github.com/isaacs/node-supervisor
```

Head back over to your browser and point it to `http://localhost:3000/user/new`—you should see something like the following screenshot:

Now, we're not going to win any design awards with this, but still, our form is up there with very little effort. Unfortunately, it doesn't do anything yet, so let's fix that right now!

Adding the create user function

The route we've declared to use—to handle the new user form—is `user.doCreate`, so we will create the `doCreate` export function in `routes/user.js`.

The bare bones of what we want to do are:

1. Take the name and e-mail address from the new user form.
2. Add the current date and time for modifiedOn and lastLogin.
3. Create the new user.
4. Save the new user to the database.
5. Confirm the save operation to the console.

We will flesh this out soon, but that's the minimum functionality we're after. We'll use the Model.create() method we looked at before, to create and save the document in one go, so add the following lines to your routes/user.js file:

```
// POST new user creation form
exports.doCreate = function(req, res){
  User.create({
    name: req.body.FullName,
    email: req.body.Email,
    modifiedOn : Date.now(),
    lastLogin : Date.now()
  }, function( err, user ){
    if(!err){
      console.log("User created and saved: " + user);
    }
  });
};
```

Remember that if the operation is successful, then the saved object is returned to the callback function. So if you were to run this successfully you could expect to see something like the following returned to the console:

```
User created and saved: { __v: 0,
  name: 'Simon Holmes',
  email: 'simon@theholmesoffice.com',
  createdOn: Sun Apr 21 2013 15:53:07 GMT+0100 (BST),
  lastLogin: Sun Apr 21 2013 15:53:07 GMT+0100 (BST),
  _id: 5173fd53aef1909b49000001,
  modifiedOn: Sun Apr 21 2013 15:53:07 GMT+0100 (BST) }
```

Note how the createdOn value has been set using the default specified in the schema, and the unique key _id has been added, created, and returned to us.

Error trapping

This is all very well and good, but what if the save operation isn't successful? Well, we'll get an error object returned that we can look out for. We will first check if that error exists, and log it to the console for now. We will then check for the error code **11000**. You may recall from *Chapter 3, Schemas and Models* that this is the error which MongoDB will return if the e-mail address already exists in the database.

Our callback function now looks like the following:

```
function( err, user ){
  if(err){
    console.log(err);
    if(err.code===11000){
      res.redirect( '/user/new?exists=true' );
    }else{
      res.redirect('/?error=true');
    }
  }else{
    // Success
    console.log("User created and saved: " + user);
  }
}
```

So if an error is thrown while creating and saving the user we'll output it to the console, and redirect the visitor to `/?error=true`, except if the error code is **11000** when we redirect the user to `/user/new?exists=true`. We could use both of these techniques to let the visitor know what has happened.

> There are several other MongoDB error codes that you can check for, allowing you to be as specific and granular as you want. You can find them in the following link:
>
> http://www.mongodb.org/about/contributors/error-codes/

Creating a user session

Now that we've error trapped, we need to do something more useful with the new user information than just log it to the console. In order to keep using the site we will need to store some of the user information in a session cookie, so that the application can tell who each visitor is. We will also set a `Boolean` session variable named `loggedIn`.

By updating the `success` section of our callback, we now have the following:

```
// Success
console.log("User created and saved: " + user);
req.session.user = { "name" : user.name, "email": user.email, "_id":
user._id };
req.session.loggedIn = true;
res.redirect( '/user' );
```

We have used the session capabilities of Express to store some useful information about the current user that we will use soon. You'll see that the final thing we do is to redirect the visitor to the user profile page /user.

> You will notice that at the time of restarting the application, all existing sessions are lost as the default Express memory store does not persist outside of the running process. This can present a problem in live environments, but can be solved quite easily by using an external memory store to hold the session data.

Displaying the confirmation page

To keep things simple, we are going to use the user profile page as the confirmation page.

For now we will have a super-simple Jade template. For this create a template /views/user-page.jade and add the following under the `block content` section:

```
h1 Mongoose Project Management
h2= name
p Email: #{email}
  h3 Actions
  ul
    li
      a(href="/project/new") Create a new project
    li
      a(href="/user/edit") Edit user info
    li
      a(href="/user/delete") Delete #{name}
    li
      a(href="/logout") Logout #{name}
```

We have also added a section for page specific navigation, allowing the user to take specific actions. We will tie these up to code as we go along.

Next add the new export function to `routes/user.js`:

```
// GET logged in user page
exports.index = function (req, res) {
  if(req.session.loggedIn === true){
    res.render('user-page', {
      title: req.session.user.name,
      name: req.session.user.name,
      email: req.session.user.email,
      userID: req.session.user._id
    })
  }else{
    res.redirect('/login');
  }
}
```

Note that we are checking to see if a user is logged in before rendering the user page template, sending it some user data from the session object. If there is no active session then the visitor will be redirected to the login page. We will create the login page when we have looked at how to use Mongoose to read data.

Try it out!

You can now save the files, restart the application, and head to `http://localhost:3000/user/new`. Try creating a few new users, and try registering a few with the same e-mail address to see the error trapping in progress. See how it works without having to do anything so mundane as creating a database? Refreshing isn't it!

Adding create project functionality

Managing projects in our application is similar to how we manage the users, so we won't go through it in great detail here. I will just point out the highlights and any differences. You can get the full code from the download that accompanies this book.

Routes

The following are the two main routes, to be added to `app.js`:

```
// PROJECT ROUTES
app.get('/project/new', project.create);      // Create new
                                               //project form
app.post('/project/new', project.doCreate);    // Create new
                                               //project action
```

New files and functions

You will need to create some new files and functions to build the functionality, and to display it in the browser. As a starting point you'll be looking at the following files:

- Routing: You will need to create a new controller file `/routes/project.js` and two new functions `exports.create()` and `exports.doCreate()`

- Display: You will need to create a new template file `views/project-form.jade`

At this point we will not be displaying the new project information on a webpage, just outputting to a `console.log`. Before we can view it on a page we need to learn how to query the database to find the correct information, as project data is not stored in a session in the same way as the user information.

Summary

In this chapter, we have learned how to use the default methods provided by Mongoose to create and save new database entries, based on our schemas and models. We have seen that you can run a quick single command, or have greater control and flexibility through issuing a series of separate commands.

In our project, we have now added the ability to create users and projects.

Coming up in the next chapter, we're going to look at how to use Mongoose to query the database, to find the data we want and use it to populate a web page.

6
Interacting with Data – Reading, Querying, and Finding

So we've seen how Mongoose provides simple static methods for adding data to the database. Now let's see what Mongoose offers to help us find the data we want by querying the database and reading the data back into model instances in our application.

In this chapter we will:

- Learn about the built-in options for querying MongoDB through Mongoose
- Get practical by updating our application, letting us find individual users, individual projects and lists of projects
- Extend on the default functionality by creating our own static method

Approaches to find and read data

Mongoose offers many ways of querying data, but much like what we saw in *Chapter 5, Interacting with Data – Creation*, there is more than one way to execute your command.

- Using the QueryBuilder interface to build a query step by step before executing it at a specific point in your code
- Immediately with a single command

Here we have the best of both worlds. Using the QueryBuilder interface offers a greater level of flexibility and complexity, whereas the immediate execution option gives us a nice and easy way to quickly run simple queries.

There are a number of static model methods provided by Mongoose to assist in the bulk of `find` operations, including `Model.find`, `Model.findOne`, and `Model.findById`. We will look at these static model methods in more detail very soon, and we'll also see how we can create our own.

Using the QueryBuilder

Mongoose provides a simple QueryBuilder interface for when you want to build up the query over multiple steps before executing it at a certain point in your code. Look at the example in the following snippet:

```
var myQuery = User.find({'name' : 'Simon Holmes'});
myQuery.where('age').gt(18);
myQuery.sort('-lastLogin');
myQuery.select('_id name email');
myQuery.exec(function (err, users){
  if (!err){
    console.log(users); // output array of users found
  }
});
```

You can probably figure out what this code is doing. Assuming we already have a compiled model called `User`, we are looking for all users whose name is "Simon Holmes" and who are older than 18 years. We want to order them by `lastLogin` in a descending order (that is, most recent first), and only return the three document fields `_id`, `name`, and `email`. When the query result is returned, we do something with it in a callback function passed to the `.exec` call.

If you prefer you can chain the commands using dot syntax. The earlier code could be rewritten using the dot syntax method as in the following:

```
User.find({'name' : 'Simon Holmes'})
.where('age').gt(18)
.sort('-lastLogin')
.select('_id name email')
.exec(function (err, users){
  if (!err){
    console.log(users); // output array of users found
  }
});
```

Or we can create a combination of the previous two:

```
var myQuery = User.find({'name' : 'Simon Holmes'})
.where('age').gt(18)
.sort('-lastLogin')
.select('_id name email');
// do some other operations
// and then...
myQuery.exec(function (err, users){
  if (!err){
    console.log(users); // output array of users found
  }
});
```

There are far too many options for the QueryBuilder interface for us to cover in this book. Many of the query capabilities of MongoDB have been given helper methods in Mongoose. So there are all types of queries you can put together, such as geospatial distance queries for map data, and skipping and limiting records to perform the pagination of results.

Single query operation

The QueryBuilder interface is great for putting together complex queries and requests. It helps the code maintain better readability and is easy to understand when you come back to the code after a few months. Sometimes however, all you need is a pretty simple query that will be perfectly readable if you just format your code nicely.

This is where we use a single-query operation. The construct for a single find operation is the following:

```
Model.find(conditions, [fields], [options], [callback])
```

Tips and gotchas

In this construct, fields and options are both optional, but if you want to specify options then you must specify fields, even if you send it as null.

Mongoose will run the callback function when the operation has been completed. If no callback function is defined then the query will not be executed. It can however be called explicitly by using the .exec() method we saw earlier.

Let's look at some examples. The most basic approach, supplying just the conditions and the callback function, is as follows:

```
User.find(
   {'name' : 'Simon Holmes'}, // users called Simon Holmes
   function (err, users){
      if (!err){console.log(users);}
});
```

Also specifying which fields we want to be returned as in the following:

```
User.find(
   {'name' : 'Simon Holmes'}, // users called Simon Holmes
   'name email', // returning just the name and email fields
   function (err, users){
      if (!err){console.log(users);}
});
```

Or using the options to specify a sort order as in the following code snippet:

```
User.find(
   {'name' : 'Simon Holmes'}, // users called Simon Holmes
   null, // returning all fields in model
   {sort : {lastLogin : -1}}, // sorted by lastLogin descending
   function (err, users){
      if (!err){console.log(users);}
});
```

Static helper methods – finding data

Each of the two approaches makes use of a number of static helper methods that Mongoose provides. Some of the static methods that can use both approaches are as follows:

- `Model.find(query)` to return an array of instances matching the query
- `Model.findOne(query)` to return the first instance found that matches the query
- `Model.findById(ObjectID)` to return a single instance matching the given ObjectID

As we have already seen, there are various parameters that can be added to the `Model.find` method. The same applies for each of these static methods.

We need to use each of them in our project, as well as creating our own static method. So let's learn by doing.

CRUD – reading user and project data

Now we're going to go through the main three static methods for a specific use case in our application. We'll also wrap one of these inside a custom static method that we are going to create.

findOne() – finding a single user

First up, let's add the ability for a returning user to log in. At this moment we are not using any type of authentication. This is intentional as there is a plethora of options out there for password hashing and encryption, using OAuth or social network accounts. While there are several node modules available to help with this, it will just prove a distraction while we're building the bare bones of our app. For now, while we're putting it together we'll stick to just entering an e-mail address to enable us to switch between users.

The routes we're going to use are in the following code snippet:

```
app.get('/login', user.login);          // Login form
app.post('/login', user.doLogin);        // Login action
```

Login form

The first step is to create the login form—which we'll keep simple for now. So we need to create a new file view/login-form.jade with the following content:

```
h1= title
form(id="formUserLogin", method="post", action="")
  label(for="Email") Email
  input(type="email", name="Email", id="Email")
  input(type="submit", value="Login")
p Or new users can
  a(href="/user/new") sign up
```

And we need to create the corresponding controller in routes/user.js.

```
// GET login page
exports.login = function (req, res) {
  res.render('login-form', {title: 'Log in'})
}
```

Login action

The second step is to create the action itself. What we are aiming to achieve with this action is as follows

1. Check that the Email field from the form exists and contains a value.

2. Try to find a database entry with that e-mail address.

3. If the user doesn't exist, then:

    1. Send visitor back to the login screen.

4. If the user does exist, then:

    1. Return their name, e-mail address, and unique ID.

    2. Save the details to the session.

    3. Output the user object to the console so that we can see what's going on.

    4. Redirect to the user profile page /user.

Translating this to JavaScript will result in the following code that we need to add to routes/user.js. We are going to use the findOne() method as there should only be one entry in the database with this e-mail address, as Mongoose has told MongoDB that it should be a unique field. This will speed up the query operation as it returns back with the first match, rather than continuing the search to look for others.

```
// POST login page
exports.doLogin = function (req, res) {
  if (req.body.Email) {
    User.findOne(
      {'email' : req.body.Email},
      '_id name email',
      function(err, user) {
        if (!err) {
          if (!user){
            res.redirect('/login?404=user');
          }else{
            req.session.user = {
              "name" : user.name,
              "email": user.email,
              "_id": user._id
            };
            req.session.loggedin = "true";
            console.log('Logged in user: ' + user);
            res.redirect( '/user' );
```

```
        }
      };
    } else {
      res.redirect('/login?404=error');
    }
  });
  };
  } else {
    res.redirect('/login?404=error');
  }
};
```

See how in the `User.findOne` function we are sending through three parameters:

- The data object to query the database
- The data keys we want to be returned
- The callback function for when the database has finished looking

The rest should be fairly easy to follow. Even if you're not familiar with using sessions in Express, the syntax makes the code nice and easy to understand.

We already created the `/user` page in the previous section, so we're good to go!

Housekeeping – adding homepage links

Let's take a quick moment to make our lives easier and add the `sign up` and `login` links to the homepage of our app. In `views/index.jade` add the following links:

```
ul
  li
    a(href="/login") Login
  li
    a(href="/user/new") Sign up
```

Try it out!

Restart your app and head over to `http://localhost:3000` in your browser once again. From here you can test out the new links and add new users and log in as a different user.

find() – finding a list of projects and returning JSON to AJAX

If you are creating an API or just want an endpoint for an AJAX call, then you really want to respond to a request with JSON, not HTML.

Mongoose and Express work together nicely to make this really simple for us. In a nutshell, once we have retrieved the Mongoose data object from a query, we can use the res.json() method of Express to return this response as JSON, instead of being rendered as an HTML file through a templating engine.

Let's put together a useful example for this. On the user profile page we really want to have a list of projects that the logged in user has created. We are going to make this happen with an AJAX call.

Creating a new static find method

A neat feature of Mongoose is the ability to define your own static methods to suit your needs. You do this *after* the schema is declared, but *before* the model is compiled. After the model is compiled, you will be able to use your new static method in the same way that you use the pre-built methods.

Let's use a real example that we need for our code to see how this works. In our projectSchema we store the _id of the user who created it as createdBy. We want to do a find() operation on this to return an array of instances.

So, here's how we define a static method by adding it to the statics collection of the schema. Add this static method to model/db.js, again *after* the schema is declared, but *before* the model is compiled.

```
projectSchema.statics.findByUserID = function (userid, callback) {
  this.find(
    { createdBy: userid },
    '_id projectName',
    {sort: 'modifiedOn'}
    callback);
}
```

This creates a new model method for us, so that we will now be able to call Model.findByUserID(userid,callback) in the same way that we called Model.findOne when creating the login functionality earlier.

Inside our method we are calling the `Model.find` method, passing it four parameters:

- Query object
- Items to select and return
- Options (in this case a sort order)
- A callback function

All being well, this will return an array of Project instances that were created by a single user. This will look something like the following:

```
[ {  _id: 51412597e8e6d3e35c000001, projectName: 'First project' },
  { projectName: 'Another test', _id: 515c6b47596acf8e35000001 },
  { projectName: 'Project 3', _id: 517d2592ebc5782c6a000001 } ]
```

Setting up the route

Now that we have the needed method in place, we need to set up the routing and controller, so that we can use a URL to call it. First off, let's add the route to `app.js` to define the URL.

```
app.get('/project/byuser/:userid', project.byUser);   // Projects
                                                //created by a user
```

Now we can set the controller up in `routes/project.js`. We want this new controller to do the following:

1. Check that a `userid` has been sent.
2. Call our `findByUserID` method, passing it the `userid`.
3. Pass a callback to output the returned data set as JSON.

We will also error trap and console log along the way, so that we can keep track of what is going on. So, add the following to `routes/projects.js` and we'll take a look at what's going on:

```
// GET Projects by UserID
exports.byUser = function (req, res) {
  console.log("Getting user projects");
  if (req.params.userid){
    Project.findByUserID(
      req.params.userid,
      function (err, projects) {
        if(!err){
          console.log(projects);
```

```
                res.json(projects);
            }else{
              console.log(err);
              res.json({"status":"error", "error":"Error finding
    projects"});
            }
        })
    }else{
        console.log("No user id supplied");
        res.json({"status":"error", "error":"No user id supplied"});
    }
};
```

The error trapping and logging to the console makes this piece of code look longer than it is. The real trick on this one is using `res.json` to return the output as JSON, instead of rendering HTML.

Updating the view

We're going to be lazy now and use jQuery to manage our AJAX call and HTML injection. In the head section of `views/layout.jade`, add jQuery and support for an inline JavaScript block that we'll call `headjs`:

```
script(src="//ajax.googleapis.com/ajax/libs/jquery/1.9.1/jquery.min.
js")
block headjs
```

Next update `views/user-page.jade` to use this new `headjs` section. We need to take the user ID passed to the page and turn it into a JavaScript variable. We'll put the rest of our JavaScript in an external file so that it can be cached. Here's how to do it:

```
block headjs
  script()
    var userID = "#{userID}";
  script(src="/javascripts/user.js")
```

Finally, we'll add an additional piece of HTML into which we will inject the list of projects:

```
h3 My projects
ul#myprojects
  li loading...
```

Building the AJAX call

Okay, we're nearly there. We just need to create the jQuery AJAX call to tie it all together.

Create a new text file `user.js` in `public/javascripts/` with the following content:

```
$(document).ready(function(){
  var strHTMLOutput = '';
  $.ajax('/project/byuser/' + userID, {
    dataType: 'json',
    error: function(){
      console.log("ajax error :(");
    },
    success: function (data) {
      if (data.length > 0) {
        if (data.status && data.status === 'error'){
          strHTMLOutput = "<li>Error: " + data.error + "</li>";
        } else {
          var intItem,
              totalItems = data.length,
              arrLI = [];
          for (intItem = totalItems - 1; intItem >= 0; intItem--) {
            arrLI.push('<a href="/project/' + data[intItem]._id + '">'
+ data[intItem].projectName + "</a>");
          }
          strHTMLOutput = "<li>" + arrLI.join('</li><li>') + "</li>";
        }
      }else{
        strHTMLOutput = "<li>You haven't created any projects yet</
li>";
      }
      $('#myprojects').html(strHTMLOutput);
    }
  });
});
```

I won't break down the finer points of a jQuery AJAX call, but what we've just done is:

- Waited until the DOM has loaded
- Made an AJAX call to the route `/project/byuser/` adding `userID` to the end for our export function to use

- If we get a successful response

  ○ Loop through the array of instances making each one an `<li>`

  ○ Inject the resulting HTML into the page

Try it out!

Restart your app and head over to `http://localhost:3000` in your browser. Either log in as an existing user, or create a new user and a few projects. On the user profile page—`http://localhost:3000/user`—you should now see a list of projects as shown in the following screenshot:

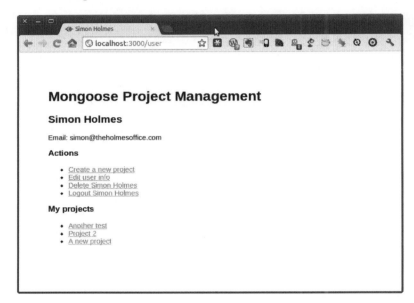

findById() – finding a single project

Something is missing so far, we don't have a page displaying the data for a single project. Let's add that and take a look at the `model.findById` method as we go.

Route setup

To work with a URL like the following:

```
http://localhost:3000/project/5182067c9756e3036c000003
```

This is the route we need to use:

```
app.get('/project/:id', project.displayInfo);      // Display
                                                //project info
```

So we need to add some code to routes/project.js. We're doing a quick authentication check here, but only at a development environment level. We are only checking to see if a user is logged in, not that they have specific permissions to access this project. After that, assuming the id field has been passed as a URL parameter, we will use the Project.findById method to—well—find the project by ID!

```
// GET project info
exports.displayInfo = function(req, res) {
  console.log("Finding project _id: " + req.params.id);
  if (req.session.loggedin !== "true"){
    res.redirect('/login');
  }
  else {
    if (req.params.id) {
      Project.findById( req.params.id, function(err,project) {
        if(err){
          console.log(err);
          res.redirect('/user?404=project');
        }else{
          console.log(project);
          res.render('project-page', {
            title: project.projectName,
            projectName: project.projectName,
            tasks: project.tasks,
            createdBy: project.createdBy,
            projectID: req.params.id
          });
        }
      });
    }else{
      res.redirect('/user');
    }
  }
};
```

As you can see, ignoring the console logs and error traps, we are sending two parameters to our new static Project.findById method. We're passing it the _id of the project that we have parsed from the URL parameters, and a callback function whose main purpose is to send the project details to the view.

Creating the view

The view itself will be quite simple for now. We just need the following content in the `block content` section of a new view `views/project-page.jade`.

```
h1 Mongoose Project Management
h2= projectName
p Created by: #{createdBy}
p Tasks: !{escape(tasks).replace(/\n/g, '<br/>')}
```

The last line in the code is just a way of substituting line breaks in the list of tasks with `<br />` tags.

Summary

In this chapter, we have learned how to query MongoDB through Mongoose by returning single instances and arrays of instances. We have seen how to run quick single command operations and also how to build more complex queries.

We have added a number of different approaches to our MongoosePM project, which includes returning JSON directly to an AJAX request. On top of all of this we have used the ability of Mongoose to create custom static methods to make it easy to get exactly what we want.

In the next chapter, we are going to take a look at updating data, so that we can allow users to change their profiles and projects.

7
Interacting with Data – Updating

In the previous chapter, we've seen how to put data in and read it back out. It's time to see how to change the existing data. In this chapter, we will look at the three built-in static model methods that help us update in one command, and the instance method we can use to save a document following a find operation.

By the end of this chapter, you will have a good understanding of how to use the different approaches, and which one is appropriate to different scenarios. You will also have added the ability to make edits to the logged in user, update a project's information, and log the last time a user logged in.

Model helper methods

There are three static methods for updating data in a single go:

- `update()`: This method updates matching documents in the database without returning them

- `findOneAndUpdate()`: This method has the same approach as `findOne` that we looked at earlier, but writes the updates to the database before returning the found instance to the callback

- `findByIdAndUpdate()`: This method is the same as `findOneAndUpdate`, but expects a unique ID instead of query object

Building the commands

Each of these methods can take the following four arguments:

- `conditions`: These are the query conditions (or `_id` for `findByIdAndUpdate`) used to find documents to update
- `update`: This is an object containing the fields and values to set
- `options`: This is an object specifying options for this operation (see more details about this in just a moment)
- `callback`: This is the function to run after a successful operation

The options differ depending on the call made. The update() method has one set of options you can set, and the find methods share another set of options.

The `update()` options are as follows:

- `safe`: Specifies whether errors should be returned to the callbacks. Can be true or false, the default value is the value set in the schema, if this was not explicitly set in the schema it defaults to true.
- `upsert`: Specifies whether to create the document if no matching document exists. Can be true or false, the default value is false.
- `multi`: Specifies whether multiple documents should be updated. Can be true or false, the default value is false.
- `strict`: Specifies whether only data defined in the schema will be saved, regardless of whether anything additional was passed to the model constructor. Can be true or false, the default value is true.

The options for the `findByIdAndUpdate()` and `findOneAndUpdate()` methods are as follows:

- `new`: Specifies whether to return the modified document rather than the original. Can be true or false, the default value is true.
- `upsert`: Specifies whether to create the document if it doesn't exist. Can be true or false, the default value is false.
- `sort`: If some documents are found, sets the sort order to choose which one to update. This should be a JavaScript object.
- `select`: This sets the document fields to return. This is specified as a string.

Which method to choose

My main rule of thumb is to only use `update()` when intentionally updating multiple documents. Remember to set `multi` to `true` in the options if you want to update multiple documents in one operation. Although in some cases you may decide to use it for updating a single document when you don't need to use a return object.

If you are going to use the data after updating, I recommend using one of the `find` methods. This will ensure that what you're using in your application is exactly what is in the database, so any problems can be quickly identified.

The catch

All three of these methods offer a fantastically quick way of doing things. But there is a catch. Any default values, validation, middleware, or setters applied to your schema will *not* be applied.

So, whenever you want to use any of these things, you'll have to go back to a standard practice of find document, modify the data, and then save it.

The three-step find-edit-save approach

This approach requires a few more steps and a bit more code than the helper methods but is more fully featured. The `save()` command accepts only one parameter, a callback function to run once the save has completed. This callback function can pass an error or return the saved object. Look at the following example:

```
// 1: FIND the record
User.findOne(
  {email : 'simon@theholmesoffice.com'},
  function(err, user) {
    if(!err){
      // 2: EDIT the record
      user.name = "Simon";
      // 3: SAVE the record
      user.save(function(err,user){
        console.log('User saved:', user);
      });
    }
  };
);
```

As you can see there is a bit more code required, and there's also an extra callback level. However, the code remains pretty simple to follow. To make it even easier, you can also define the callbacks as separate functions. We'll see this later.

CRUD – editing users and projects

While we haven't looked at validation yet, knowing the earlier "catch" will be very helpful while handling data interactions. We should bear it in mind when building our form handling actions, and use the correct methods wherever possible so that we don't have to rewrite them later.

Tracking user login

When a user logs in, we want to update the `lastLogin` date. We don't need any validation as we are setting the single field ourselves on the server, and we don't need the object returned from the database. We also know we are going to get the correct instance as our query object will be for the unique `_id` field, so we can use the `update()` method.

User login is currently handled by the `doLogin` function in `routes/user.js`. The section of the function that handles a successful login looks like the following:

```
req.session.user = { "name" : user.name, "email": user.email,
"_id": user._id };
req.session.loggedIn = true;
console.log('Logged in user: ' + user);
res.redirect( '/user' );
```

So let's update that chunk of code with a new `update()` function to set the `lastLogin` in the database:

```
req.session.user = { "name" : user.name, "email": user.email, "_id":
user._id };
req.session.loggedIn = true;
console.log('Logged in user: ' + user);
User.update(
  {_id:user._id},
  { $set: {lastLogin: Date.now()} },
  function(){
    res.redirect( '/user' );
});
```

Simple, hey? Now when a user logs in we set the `lastLogin` date, but leave everything else unchanged.

Editing the current user

Now we're at the point where it will be useful if a user can edit their profile once they have logged in. So let's set that up.

Routes in use

These are the two routes we'll be using, one to display the form, and the other to handle the submission of the form:

```
app.get('/user/edit', user.edit);        // Edit current user form
app.post('/user/edit', user.doEdit);     // Edit current user action
```

Setting up the form

We already have a user form that is used for signing up. As we're not adding anything else to a user profile at the moment, it makes sense to re-use. The first thing to do is modify `views/user-form.jade` to display the `name` and `email` values sent to it from the controllers.

```
h1= title
label(for="FullName") Full name
input(type="text", name="FullName", id="FullName", value="#{name}")
label(for="Email") Email
input(type="email", name="Email", id="Email", value="#{email}")
input(type="submit", value="#{buttonText}")
```

Setting up the controllers

With the change to the jade template earlier, we will have stopped our user signup form from working, as it is expecting variables that we are not sending. So in the `routes/user.js` file, update `exports.create` to send the empty variables:

```
exports.create = function(req, res){
  res.render('user-form', {
    title: 'Create user',
    name: "",
    email: "",
    buttonText: "Join!"
  });
};
```

We can use this function as the basis for our user edit form, by adding the following controller into `routes/user.js`:

```
// GET user edit form
exports.edit = function(req, res){
  if (req.session.loggedIn !== true){
    res.redirect('/login');
  }else{
    res.render('user-form', {
      title: 'Edit profile',
      _id: req.session.user._id,
      name: req.session.user.name,
      email: req.session.user.email,
      buttonText: "Save"
    });
  }
};
```

As you can see, here we are passing the current user's name and e-mail address from the session object to the view.

Committing the edit

Further down the line we will want to add validation to this submission. So we can't use any of the shorthand helper methods for updating. We need to use the three-step approach:

1. Find our user by the unique ID held in the session.
2. Change the name and e-mail to the values sent in the form.
3. Save the changes.

In `routes/user.js`, we need to add the following controller:

```
// POST user edit form
exports.doEdit = function(req, res) {
  if (req.session.user._id) {
    User.findById( req.session.user._id,
      function (err, user) {
        if(err){
          console.log(err);
          res.redirect( '/user?error=finding');
        } else {
          user.name = req.body.FullName;
          user.email = req.body.Email;
```

```
        user.modifiedOn = Date.now();
        user.save(function (err) {
          if(!err){
            console.log('User updated: ' + req.body.FullName);
            req.session.user.name = req.body.FullName;
            req.session.user.email = req.body.Email;
            res.redirect( '/user' );
          }
        });
      }
    }
  );
};
};
```

Note that the `save` option does not return the updated document from the database, but you could use the user variable if you needed to, as it should contain the same data.

There are a few `if` conditions and callbacks in this code, but hopefully you can follow through the separate steps and see how it all ties together. Another option that you may find makes your code easier to read and follow is to make each section a separate function that is invoked from the relevant callback. For example see the following code:

```
exports.doEdit = function(req, res) {
  if (req.session.user._id) {
    User.findById( req.session.user._id,
      function (err, user) {
        doEditSave (req, res, err, user);
      }
    );
  }
};

var doEditSave = function(req, res, err, user) {
  if(err){
    console.log(err);
    res.redirect( '/user?error=finding');
  } else {
    user.name = req.body.FullName;
    user.email = req.body.Email;
    user.modifiedOn = Date.now();
    user.save(
```

```
        function (err, user) {
          onEditSave (req, res, err, user);
        }
      );
    }
};

var onEditSave = function (req, res, err, user) {
  if(err){
    console.log(err);
    res.redirect( '/user?error=saving');
  } else {
    console.log('User updated: ' + req.body.FullName);
    req.session.user.name = req.body.FullName;
    req.session.user.email = req.body.Email;
    res.redirect( '/user' );
  }
};
```

Editing projects

The approach to take for editing projects is very similar to what we have done for users. We won't cover it here in detail, but you can either download the source code available with this book, or have a go at setting it up yourself.

Remember that we pass the _id through URL parameters for projects, not in the session like we do for users.

This is because we need the user information on all pages to check that they are logged in and have access to view whatever they have requested. Project specific data is only accessed on a few pages, and a user might skip from project to project, so passing the value through the URL makes most sense.

Here are the highlights of what is required in the following sections:

Routes

These are the two main routes to be added to the app.js file:

```
app.get('/project/edit/:id', project.edit);        // Edit selected
                                                   //project form
app.post('/project/edit/:id', project.doEdit);     // Edit selected
                                                   //project action
```

New files and functions

You will need to create some new files and functions to build the functionality, and to display it in the browser. As a starting point you'll be looking at the following files:

- Routing: Inside the controller file `/routes/project.js` you will need to modify `exports.create()` and create two new functions `exports.edit()` and `exports.doEdit()`.

- Display: You will need to update the template file `views/project-form.jade` to accept and display values from variables.

Summary

In this chapter, we have learned how to modify existing data using Mongoose. We have seen that there are some very simple methods we can use, but that this simplicity comes at a price. The price in this case is that defaults, validation, and middleware are not applied. We have also seen that we can use a more traditional three-step find-edit-save approach within Mongoose.

Following this theory we moved onto the practice and added to our MongoosePM project, making `user` and `project` information updatable, and updated the login script to record a timestamp of when the user logged in.

Coming up in the next chapter we will be learning about the last of the four CRUD cornerstones, deletion.

8
Interacting with Data – Deleting

We have learned about Creating, Reading, and Updating data using Mongoose. Now it is time to look at the final CRUD operation: **deleting**.

In this chapter we will:

- Learn how to delete multiple documents in one operation
- Learn how to delete a single document
- Put this knowledge into action by adding the functionality to delete a user account

By the end of this chapter, you will be familiar with the different approaches you can take to delete data, and when it is best to use each one. You will also have added the ability to delete users and projects from your MongoosePM application.

Deleting data

By now it will probably come as no surprise that there are a few different methods for deleting data. The methods are:

- `remove()`: This method deletes one or more documents from the collection
- `findOneAndRemove()`: This method finds a single document based on a query object and removes it, passing it to the callback function on successful completion
- `findByIdAndRemove()`: This method is the same as the `findOneAndRemove` method, except that it finds a document based on a provided document ID

The `remove()` method can be used in two ways: as a model method, or as an instance method. When using it as a model method, you pass it a query object and it will remove the matching documents. For example:

```
User.remove({ name : /Simon/ } , function (err){
  if (!err){
    // all users with 'Simon' in their name were deleted
  }
});
```

To use the `remove()` method as an instance method you operate it after a find operation once you have results returned. For example:

```
User.findOne({ email : 'simon@theholmesoffice.com'} ,
  function (err,user){
    if (!err){
      user.remove( function(err){
        // First user with matching email address was removed
      });
    }
});
```

Be careful when using <Model>.remove() (where <model> is the model name). If you specify an empty query or just a callback—like you would when using the instance method—then all the documents in the collection will be removed.

Both the `findByIdAndRemove()` and `findOneAndRemove()` methods accept options and can return the deleted document to the callback. We're going to use the `findByIdAndRemove` method shortly. So let's have a look at `findOneAndRemove` instead. The accepted parameters are as follows:

- **Query object**: This is for a document to find and remove.
- **Options**: This optional parameter is an object with two possibilities:
  - ○ `sort`: set the sort order in case multiple docs are found
  - ○ `select`: set the document fields to return in the object to the callback
- **Callback**: This optional parameter This returns either an error or the deleted document.

Here's a quick example:

```
User.findOneAndRemove(
  {name : /Simon/},
```

```
        {sort : 'lastLogin', select : 'name email'},
        function (err, user){
          if (!err) {
            console.log(user.name + " removed");
            // Simon Holmes removed
          };
        }
    );
```

Here we search for users whose name contain `Simon`, and order them by the date they last logged in, before removing the user who hasn't logged in for the longest time. Once removed, we send their name and e-mail address to the callback to output confirmation of the deletion.

CRUD – deleting user and projects

That's the theory, so let's see it in action and let a user delete their account. To follow the approach we've been taking through this application, we'll have a page displaying a form and a form handler.

The routes in `app.js` that we'll use for this are:

```
app.get('/user/delete', user.confirmDelete);
                                        // delete current user form
app.post('/user/delete', user.doDelete);
                                        // Delete current user action
```

The "Are you sure" page

Before a user deletes the account we want to ask them to confirm this, in case they clicked on the link by accident. So we create a new view as `views/user-delete-form.jade`:

```
h1= title
p #{name}, are you sure you want to permanently delete your
account? The email address on this account is #{email}
form(id="formUserDelete", method="post", action="")
  input(type="hidden", name="_id", id="_id", value="#{_id}")
  input(type="submit", value="Yes, please delete it!")
```

And create a controller to map it to the route in `routes/user.js`:

```
// GET user delete confirmation form
exports.confirmDelete = function(req, res){
  res.render('user-delete-form', {
```

```
    title: 'Delete account',
    _id: req.session.user._id,
    name: req.session.user.name,
    email: req.session.user.email
  });
};
```

Deleting the user

Now we get to the business end and delete the user, using `Model.findByIdAndRemove()`. In `routes/user.js`, add the following `doDelete` exports function.

```
// POST user delete form
exports.doDelete = function(req, res) {
  if (req.body._id) {
    User.findByIdAndRemove(
      req.body._id,
      function (err, user) {
        if(err){
          console.log(err);
          return res.redirect('/user?error=deleting');
        }
        console.log("User deleted:", user);
        clearSession(req.session, function () {
          res.redirect('/');
        });
      }
    );
  }
};
```

Here we are simply taking the unique ID of the user as passed through the form, finding it in the database, and deleting the entry. Once deleted, we log the user record to the console so that we can verify it, and then we need to make sure that the user is logged out of the system and sent to the homepage.

We need to add an extra function called `clearSession` to do this, as this isn't the only place we'll need to log out a user. Add the following to `routes/user.js`:

```
var clearSession = function(session, callback){
  session.destroy();
  callback();
};
```

Improving on this

If you want to try something else, you could add to this function by deleting all projects created by the deleted user.

Deleting individual projects

The approach to take for deleting projects is very similar to what we have done for users. We won't cover it here in detail, but you can either download the source code available with this book, or have a go at setting it up yourself.

Following are the highlights of what is required:

Routes

These are the two main routes, to be added to `app.js`:

```
app.get('/project/delete/:id', project.confirmDelete);
                                //Delete selected project form
app.post('/project/delete/:id', project.doDelete);    // Delete
                                //selected project action
```

New files and functions

You will need to create some new files and functions to build the functionality, and to display it in the browser. As a starting point you'll be looking at the following files:

- Routing: Inside the controller file `/routes/project.js` you will need to create two new functions `exports.delete()` and `exports.doDelete()`.

- Display: You will need to create a new template file `views/project-delete-form.jade` to ask the user for confirmation.

Summary

In this chapter, we have learned how to delete database records using Mongoose methods. We then applied this knowledge to our project and added the ability for a user to delete their profile.

This brings us to the end of the data interaction CRUD section, so you should now have a good idea of how to do most things you want to with data in your applications.

Coming up in the next chapter, we're going to look at validation and see how Mongoose can help us maintain data integrity.

9
Validating Data

An important part of any application that takes data entered by a user is data integrity. In this chapter, we are going to look at different ways of validating data before it is saved to the database. We will look at the built-in Mongoose validators, and also how to add custom validation.

By the end of this chapter, you will understand the different approaches to data validation with Mongoose, and will have added validation to create and update sections of our MongoosePM application.

Mongoose validation – the basics

In Mongoose, validation is set at the schema level. Remember how in our `userSchema` we have this for the `email` field:

```
email: { type: String, unique: true }
```

The `unique: true` part is a type of validation that Mongoose passes directly through to MongoDB. The other types of validation we are about to look at are set in the same place, but are handled by Mongoose before it goes anywhere near the database; unless of course, you have a type of validation where you specifically choose to check against something in the database.

Default validators

Mongoose provides some common validators to get us started. We'll look at them in this chapter. Some of these are for specific SchemaTypes, which we'll get to know in a moment, but there is one that can be used on all SchemaTypes.

All SchemaTypes

There is one validator that can be used by any SchemaType, named **required**. This will return a validation error if no data is given to a data object with this property. It is super-easy to use. If we want to add it to `email` in our `userSchema` we simply need to update the line as follows:

```
email: { type: String, unique: true, required: true }
```

Number SchemaType

Number items in your schema have built-in **min** and **max** validators, for declaring lower and upper boundaries. They are also simple to apply. See the following for example:

```
var teenSchema = new Schema({
   age : {type: Number, min: 13, max:19}
});
```

This will return a validation error if you try to save an instance of `teenSchema` with an age value of less than 13, or higher than 19.

String SchemaType

String items in your schema have two other built-in validators:

- **match**: This validator is for matching against a regular expression
- **enum**: This validator is for checking against a provided list of possible values

Here the `match` validator will check that the string matches the regular expression:

```
var weekdaySchema = new Schema({
   day : {type: String, match: /^(mon|tues|wednes|thurs|fri)day$/i}
});
```

Here the `enum` validator will check that the string is one of the values in the `weekdays` array:

```
var weekdays = ['monday', 'tuesday', 'wednesday', 'thursday',
'friday'];
var weekdaySchema = new Schema({
   day : {type: String,  enum: weekdays}
});
```

Understanding validation errors

When we have been creating, editing, and saving data in our project, we have been using a callback function containing two parameters: an error object and the returned data object. So far we have generally been ignoring the error object and just been saving the data, for example:

```
user.save(function (err, user) {
  if(err){
    console.log(err)
  } else { ...
```

It is in the `err` object that we receive the Mongoose validation errors. The error object will contain a top-level message and name, and a collection of specific errors. Each of these errors give an individual `message`, `name`, `path`, and `type` object. A typical validation failure looks like the following when sent to the console:

```
{ message: 'Validation failed',
  name: 'ValidationError',
  errors:
   { email:
      { message: 'Validator "required" failed for path email',
        name: 'ValidatorError',
        path: 'email',
        type: 'required' },
     name:
      { message: 'Validator "required" failed for path name',
        name: 'ValidatorError',
        path: 'name',
        type: 'required' } } }
```

Knowing the structure of the returned error object helps us to identify the exact reason for the validation failure and send a relevant error message to the user.

To output just a summary to the console, you could loop through the error objects with the following code snippet:

```
if(err){
  Object.keys(err.errors).forEach(function(key) {
    var message = err.errors[key].message;
    console.log('Validation error for "%s": %s', key, message);
  });
}
```

This would result in a much more manageable output, which is as follows:

```
Validation error for "email": Validator "required" failed for path
email
Validation error for "name": Validator "required" failed for path
name
```

Doing it your way – create custom validation

Mongoose offers a number of different ways to create custom validators.

Single function – no custom error message

If you only need one piece of validation for a given data item, you can simply specify a function and return `true` if the validation is passed, and `false` if it fails.

For example, if we want our usernames to be at least five characters long, we can create a function like the following:

```
var lengthValidator = function(val) {
  if (val && val.length >= 5){
    return true;
  }
  return false;
};
```

The function is then referenced in our schema using the `validate` key:

```
name: {type: String, required: true, validate: lengthValidator }
```

This is a very quick and easy way of adding custom validation. It is fine if you just want to check if its okay or not okay as it is reported as an error, but in the error collection the error `type` comes through as `undefined`.

Returning a custom error message

If you want a bit more feedback and granularity to your error trapping then it's useful to add a custom error message. Fortunately, Mongoose makes this pretty easy too!

Using the previous schema entry as a start point you can change the value of the `validate` entity, setting an object instead. This object has two entries:

- `validator`: This is your custom function
- `msg`: This is your custom error message

For example:

```
validate: { validator: lengthValidator, msg: 'Too short' }
```

Validating a regular expression

If you just want to validate against a regular expression, you don't have to create a function to house it. Mongoose lets you put it directly into the schema.

```
var weekdaySchema = new Schema({
  day : {type: String, validate: {validator:
/^(mon|tues|wednes|thurs|fri)day$/i, msg: 'Not a day' }
});
```

Taking the messages out of the schema

You can take the pairing of the validation function and custom message outside of the schema so that both are re-usable. This is done by defining an array that contains your validator and your message.

```
var validateLength = [lengthValidator, 'Too short' ];
var validateDay = [/^(mon|tues|wednes|thurs|fri)day$/i, 'Not a
day' ];
```

You simply reference these in your schema definitions like in the following:

```
name: {type: String, required: true, validate: validateLength }
```

Or:

```
day : {type: String, validate: validateDay }
```

An array might seem like an odd choice at the moment, but everything will become clear soon!

Using multiple re-usable validators

If you aim to make your code as re-usable as possible, then you'll want to create a few validation functions, each of which does just one thing. You can then mix and match, sharing across schemas and even different applications when you create them. Here's where that array comes in:

The code we saw beforehand is as follows:

```
var validateLength = [lengthValidator, 'Too short' ];
```

This is syntactic shorthand for the following:

```
var validateLength = [
  {validator: lengthValidator, msg: 'Too short'}
];
```

Now the array starts to make a bit more sense doesn't it? We can add further validation objects to it like in the following:

```
var validateUsername = [
  {validator: lengthValidator, msg: 'Too short'} ,
  {validator: /^[a-z]+$/i, msg: 'Letters only'}
];
```

[The *best practice* is to use the longer form, explicitly defining the object and not the syntactic shorthand. This makes your code easier to understand at a glance, and also easier to extend.]

As you can see, it's pretty easy to build up a set of re-usable validators and apply them to your schemas. There is one more way of doing this, by using the SchemaType methods:

```
userSchema.path('name').validate(lengthValidator, 'Too short');
userSchema.path('name').validate(/^[a-z]+$/i, 'Letters only');
```

Non-blocking, asynchronous validation

So far we've been looking at validation methods that run pretty much instantly, but what if we want to run an asynchronous operation such as checking against a database? Mongoose provides the ability to run an asynchronous validator to do just this. To use this you specify a validator function with a second parameter—this second parameter is a callback function that expects either `true` or `false`.

In the following example, we are using `respond` as our callback function, and checking to see whether a user record with the supplied username already exists.

```
userSchema.path('username').validate(function (value, respond) {
  User.find({username: value}, function(err, users){
    if (err){
      console.log(err);
      return respond(false);
    }
    console.log('Number found: ' + users.length);
    if (users.length) {
      respond(false); // validation failed
```

```
    } else {
      respond(true); // validation passed
    }
  })
}, 'Duplicate username');
```

Extending Mongoose validation

While the validation functions you get with Mongoose are already pretty good, you won't find everything there out-of-the-box. If you want validators for e-mail addresses, IP addresses, alphanumeric values, URLs — the list goes on — there are modules that can be installed and easily plugged in to your application. These all take advantage of Mongoose's plugin architecture, which we'll see in detail in *Chapter 11, Plugins – Reusing Code.*

Adding validation to our project

Now that we've done the theory, why not see if you can add some validation to our MongoosePM application? We're not going to walk through this here, but do try it out yourself. If you're impatient you can of course just download the source code from Packt's website. The code contains various ways of achieving the same validation, commented out for reference.

For users, try adding the following validations:

- **Name**: Make this `required`, and with a minimum length of five characters
- **Email**: Make this `required`, unique, and only allow a valid e-mail address

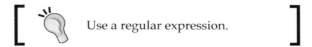 Use a regular expression.

For projects, have a go at this:

- **projectName**: Make this `required`, with a minimum length of five characters, and only accept unique values for each user

 Use an asynchronous validator.

To get the validation working for both users and projects, you will need to:

- Update the schemas to include validators
- Update the create/edit controllers to interpret the error messages
- Save the submitted data into a temporary session object
- Update the form views to display the previously entered data

If all else fails, download the source code for a few ideas!

Summary

In this chapter, we've seen how to use Mongoose to maintain the data integrity of our application. We have learned about the default validators that are available, and also learned how to use them and how to create custom validators. Within the custom validators, we've covered how to send custom error messages, add multiple validators, and run asynchronous validation. We also took a look at the error object returned when your validators find a problem with the data.

Coming up in the next chapter, we're going to take a look at complex schemas, including nested documents and referencing other schemas.

10
Complex Schemas

In this chapter, we will explore the ways in which Mongoose can help you manage more complex data models. MongoDB is not a relational database, so there are no SQL-style JOIN commands. Instead, we will introduce the concepts of **population** and **subdocuments**, exploring how they are used.

By the end of this chapter, you will understand the differences between the two, and when each type is appropriate. We will also have added examples to our MongoosePM application.

Population – references to other collections

MongoDB and Mongoose do not support JOIN commands as MongoDB is not a relational database. Mongoose gives you an elegant way to achieve similar functionality by using population.

 The concept of Population was dramatically expanded upon in Version 3.6 of Mongoose. Older versions won't support everything referenced in this chapter.

Population works by pulling information into the model you're currently using from a second model. Unlike JOIN statements, these are actually separate queries. First you retrieve your primary set of data from a collection, and once that is returned, you "populate" the required data from a secondary collection. We'll see this in some code very soon.

Defining data for population

The first step to setting up population is in the schema. Your primary schema links to the referenced model by passing an object containing the name of the model to be used and the SchemaType of the linked schema object.

In our application, there are various times when it will be useful to get the information about the person who created a specific project. Currently we store the _id of the user as a string, which we could use to manually query the users collection once we have the data back from the projects collection. Or, we could store that _id as a reference and let Mongoose do the hard work for us. Sounds preferable to me!

Remember from the first paragraph of this section: Your primary schema links to the referenced model by passing an object containing the name of the model to be used and the SchemaType of the linked schema object. So, by breaking this down, in our projectSchema we want to set the createdBy path to be:

- An object { }
- To contain the name of the model to be used—ref: 'User'
- and the SchemaType of the linked schema object—type: mongoose. Schema.Types.ObjectId

So, by putting this back together, we can change the createdBy declaration in our projectSchema like this:

```
var projectSchema = new mongoose.Schema({
  ...
  createdBy: {type: mongoose.Schema.Types.ObjectId, ref: 'User'},
  ...
});
```

> ObjectId, Number, String, and Buffer are valid SchemaTypes for using as references. You only need to declare the full Schema. Type path for ObjectId.

Here we are saying that there is a one-to-one relationship between the User model and the Project model, but populate can also work with a one-to-many relationship by specifying an array of objects. If we want to record a number of contributors to a project, we simply take what we have for the createdBy definition and put it in inside an array, like this:

```
var projectSchema = new mongoose.Schema({
  ...
  createdBy: {type: mongoose.Schema.Types.ObjectId, ref: 'User'},
```

```
contributors: [ {type: mongoose.Schema.Types.ObjectId, ref: 'User'} ]
  ,
  ...
});
```

In MongoDB a document for this schema would look something like this:

```
{ "projectName" : "Population test",
  "createdBy" : ObjectId("5126b7a1f8a44d1e32000001"),
  "_id" : ObjectId("51ac2fc4c746ba1645000002"),
  "contributors" : [
    ObjectId("5126b7a1f8a44d1e32000001"),
    ObjectId("5126b7a1f8a44d1e32000002") ] }
```

 Changing an existing schema like this can have serious impacts on the existing data and database. See the *Data management when modifying existing schemas* section towards the end of this chapter.

Saving population references

You don't have to do anything different to save a population reference, you just need to set the data and save a document the normal way. So we don't need to change our `Project.create` function at all:

```
Project.create({
  projectName: req.body.projectName,
  createdBy: req.body.userid,
  createdOn : Date.now()
}, function( err, project ){ …
```

Retrieving populated data

Just like the JOIN command you only use population when you need it. If you just want to return the project information with no mention of the creator's details then you can stick with the following:

```
Project.findById( req.params.id, function(err,project) { ...
```

In our application, however, when we display the project information page—using the `displayInfo` function in `routes/project.js`—we show the ID of the user who created the project. It would be much nicer if we could display the name and e-mail address instead.

To do this, you build a query, use the `populate` command, and then `exec()` when ready. For example:

```
Project
.findById( req.params.id)
.populate('createdBy')
.exec(function(err,project) { ...
```

This will populate with the entire user object, returning an object something like the following:

```
{ __v: 0,
  _id: 51b495e01e686ea360000002,
  createdBy:
   { __v: 0,
     _id: 5126b7a1f8a44d1e32000001,
     email: 'simon@theholmesoffice.com',
     lastLogin: Sun Aug 04 2013 07:34:21 GMT+0100 (BST),
     modifiedOn: Sun Jul 28 2013 16:32:15 GMT+0100 (BST),
     name: 'Simon Holmes',
     createdOn: Fri Feb 22 2013 00:11:13 GMT+0000 (GMT) },
  modifiedOn: Sun Jul 07 2013 16:21:50 GMT+0100 (BST),
  projectName: 'Updated project schemas',
  createdOn: Sun Jun 09 2013 15:49:04 GMT+0100 (BST) }
```

All of this information about the user is unnecessary for us here, so we can specify the individual paths that we require. As we just want the name and e-mail of the creator, we can specify the following:

```
.populate('createdBy', 'name email')
```

You can also populate multiple paths in the parent schema at once. Although, remember that each path is populated by a separate database query. If we wanted to return an array of all contributors in a project, we could add the following path to the populate call:

```
.populate('createdBy contributors')
```

But if you want to return specific paths for each of the populated items—even if they are the same—you have to chain the populate calls as shown in the following:

```
.populate('createdBy', 'name email')
.populate('contributors', 'name email')
```

This will give us back more manageable data like this object:

```
{ __v: 0,
  _id: 51b495e01e686ea360000002,
  createdBy:
   { _id: 5126b7a1f8a44d1e32000001,
     email: 'simon@theholmesoffice.com',
     name: 'Simon Holmes' },
  modifiedOn: Sun Jul 07 2013 16:21:50 GMT+0100 (BST),
  projectName: 'Updated project schemas',
  createdOn: Sun Jun 09 2013 15:49:04 GMT+0100 (BST),
  contributors: [
    { _id: 5126b7a1f8a44d1e32000001,
      email: 'simon@theholmesoffice.com',
      name: 'Simon Holmes' },
    { _id: 5126b7a1f8a44d1e32000002,
      email: 'someone@theholmesoffice.com',
      name: 'Someone Else' }
  ]
}
```

Querying to return a subset of results

When populating data with a one-to-many relationship, you may well want to return a subset just like you might with a standard `find` operation. So far we've been using syntactic shortcuts for the populate method, but Mongoose does give you the option of sending a query object for population, with the following parameters:

- `path`: This is the path to populate and is `required`.
- `select`: This is a string or object specifying which paths to return.
- `model`: This is the name of the model you want to populate from. It defaults to the reference specified in the schema if not declared here.
- `match`: This can specify query conditions.
- `options`: This can specify query options.

So if we wanted to populate a maximum of five contributors who have an e-mail address at `theholmesoffice.com`, to sort them by name and return name and `lastLogin` information we could do the following:

```
.populate({
  path: 'contributors',
  match: { email: /@theholmesoffice\.com/i },
  select: 'name lastLogin',
```

```
    options: { limit: 5, sort: 'name' }
  })
  .exec()
```

We don't want to do this right now, but it's nice to know that we could!

Populating into multiple parent items

Up to now all of our examples have been related to populating into a single-parent project. But this isn't a limitation of Mongoose. If your query on the primary collection returns multiple documents, you can easily populate into them See the following example:

```
Project
.find({ createdBy: userid }, 'projectName')
.populate('createdBy', 'name')
.exec(function(err,projects) {
  projects.forEach(function (project) {
    console.log(project.projectName + ' created by' + project.
createdBy.name);
  });
});
```

Subdocuments

Subdocuments are very similar to the ordinary documents we have been using so far. They are individual documents with their own schema. The big difference is that subdocuments are documents that are stored within a parent document, instead of a MongoDB collection of their own.

Perhaps an example will demonstrate this best. In our MongoosePM application, tasks are currently lacking in functionality as `tasks` for a given project is just a string. It would be better if a task had a distinct schema like the following:

```
var taskSchema = new mongoose.Schema({
  taskName: { type: String, required: true, validate: validateLength
},
  taskDesc: String,
  createdOn: { type: Date, default: Date.now },
  createdBy: { type: mongoose.Schema.Types.ObjectId, ref: 'User',
required: true},
  modifiedOn: Date,
  assignedTo: { type: mongoose.Schema.Types.ObjectId, ref: 'User' }
});
```

This schema looks a bit more useful right? In a relational database this would be a standalone table, and you would run joins between the project table, task table, and user table. But in a non-relational datastore, the better approach is to contain documents solely owned by a parent document, *within* the parent document. To do this, we reference the new `taskSchema` within the `projectSchema` as an array like the following:

```
var projectSchema = new mongoose.Schema({
    projectName: String,
    ...
    tasks: [taskSchema]
});
```

Hey presto, a nested schema! So what does our data look like if we use this? Each task subdocument created goes into the array of `tasks` as defined in the `projectSchema`.

```
{
    "projectName" : "Project 2",
    "tasks" : [
        "taskName" : "A task please",
        "taskDesc" : "A short description of the task",
        "createdBy" : ObjectId("5126b7a1f8a44d1e32000001"),
        "_id" : ObjectId("51ad7d6cfa492a174a000005"),
        "createdOn" : ISODate("2013-06-04T05:38:52.847Z")
    },
    {
        "createdBy" : ObjectId("5126b7a1f8a44d1e32000002"),
        "_id" : ObjectId("51ad7d80fa492a174a000006"),
        "createdOn" : ISODate("2013-06-04T05:39:12.728Z"),
        "modifiedOn" : ISODate("2013-06-04T05:39:48.553Z"),
        "taskDesc" : "A quick description of this one too",
        "taskName" : "A secondary task"
    }
    ]
}
```

 Mongoose will automatically give each subdocument a unique _id unless overridden in the schema.

Creating subdocuments

Creating subdocuments is super easy. When working with subdocuments we always have to go through the parent document. We also need to remember that each individual subdocument is a document in its own right, stored inside an array.

So if we want to add a new task to an existing project, we would need to:

1. Find the project in the database
2. Push a task object to the tasks path
3. Save the parent document.

   The code to do this looks like the following:

```javascript
Project.findById( req.body.projectID, 'tasks modifiedOn',
  function (err, project) {
    if(!err){
      project.tasks.push({
        taskName: req.body.taskName,
        taskDesc: req.body.taskDesc,
        createdBy: req.session.user._id
      });
      project.modifiedOn = Date.now();
      project.save(function (err, project){
        if(err){
          console.log('Oh dear', err);
        } else {
          console.log('Task saved: ' + req.body.taskName);
          res.redirect( '/project/' + req.body.projectID );
        }
      });
    }
  }
);
```

Saving and validation

You may have noticed in the code earlier that we don't explicitly save the new subdocument. Subdocuments are saved when their parent document is saved.

Any validator errors set in the subdocument schema are bubbled back up to the parent document, so the existing `if(err)` catches in the code are all that we need.

Retrieving subdocuments

As we have already learned, to get access to the subdocuments, you have to go through the parent document, and that subdocuments are stored as an array.

So if we want to display a list of tasks on our project page, we don't need to change any JavaScript, as our `displayInfo` function is already passing the tasks data to the Jade template. We simply need to change how tasks are interpreted in `views/project-page.jade`.

```
if tasks.length > 0
  ul
    for task in tasks
      li
        a(href="/project/#{projectID}/task/edit/#{task._id}",
title="#{task.taskDesc}") #{task.taskName}
```

Accessing a specific subdocument

As we saw earlier, each subdocument has a unique `_id` field. When you pass this to the subdocument method `.id()` that Mongoose provides, you will get the subdocument returned to you.

```
Project.findById( req.body.projectID, 'tasks modifiedOn',
  function (err, project) {
    if(!err){
      console.log(project.tasks); // array of tasks
      var thisTask = project.tasks.id(req.params.taskID);
      console.log(thisTask); // individual task document
    }});
```

This means that when you want to edit or delete a specific subdocument, you need to know the `_id` of the parent document *and* the `_id` of the subdocument. To this end, in our project there are some new routes where we will need to pass both `_id` values as URL parameters.

```
app.get('/project/:id/task/edit/:taskID', project.editTask);
app.post('/project/:id/task/edit/:taskID', project.doEditTask);
app.get('/project/:id/task/delete/:taskID',
project.confirmDeleteTask);
app.post('/project/:id/task/delete/:taskID',
project.doDeleteTask);
```

Deleting subdocuments

Mongoose couldn't make deleting subdocuments much easier for you. By chaining to the `.id()` method in the earlier code, you can add the `.remove()` method.

```
project.tasks.id(req.body.taskID).remove();
```

 As with all changes to subdocuments, a removed subdocument won't actually be deleted until the parent document is saved.

Data management when modifying existing schemas

If you have taken all of the changes outlined in this chapter and added them to your application, you'll probably notice quite early that the list of projects on the user page doesn't display. This is because we have changed the `schemaType` of `createdBy` in `projectSchema` from `String` to `ObjectId`. If you create new projects now, they will show up in the list.

In a development environment and a prototyping scenario, like we have here, this isn't a major issue as we can just add in some more temporary test data. If you're dealing with a live environment or pre-existing data that you want to use then you have to be a bit more careful when changing a schema in this way.

There are various ways you can handle this, both on the schema side and the data management side. A possible approach is to duplicate the existing schema in its entirety and changing the SchemaTypes that you need to.

To manage the data migration you could then either create a script to update all at once, or update on an ongoing "as needed" basis. If you have a large dataset, you'll probably want to favor the latter for performance reasons. However you choose to manage it, comes down to a judgment call each time based on latency, potential downtime, code complexity, and any other application specific consideration.

Summary

In this chapter, we've seen how Mongoose helps us to create and use more complex database structures. We can use nested schemas and subdocuments and also pull data from other collections. Our code examples can be used as the basis for updating our MongoosePM application with better task information and returning user details with projects. Download the code for this chapter from Packt Publishing's website to see it in greater detail.

Coming up next in the final chapter, we're going to look at how to re-use code using Mongoose plugins.

11
Plugins – Re-using Code

In this chapter, we will introduce the Mongoose plugin architecture and see how we can use it to create modular re-usable code. We will look at the syntax and how to write them and include them in our code.

By the end of this chapter, you will understand how to create and use Mongoose plugins. You will also know where to go to find existing plugins that others have written, and contribute to the community by submitting your own. You will have created some plugins in the MongoosePM application.

Reusable schema plugins

If we look at our schemas, we can see some common elements that we are repeating. For example, each of our schemas has an identical modifiedOn path, and our project and task schemas each have identical createdBy and createdOn paths.

If you're at all familiar with the DRY (Don't Repeat Yourself) principle of coding, you'll probably want to tidy these bits up and just declare them once. This is where the Mongoose plugin architecture comes in.

Creating a schema plugin

Let's start by creating a schema extension for adding createdOn and createdBy. Inside our model/db.js file, we can add the following code, preferably above the definitions for our two schemas:

```
var creationInfo = function creationInfo (schema, options) {
  schema.add({createdOn: { type: Date, default: Date.now }});
  schema.add({createdBy: { type: mongoose.Schema.Types.ObjectId, ref:
'User', required: true}});
};
```

This exposes a function that will allow us to plug in the paths createdOn and createdBy, to some of our schemas. The construct might look a little strange, but is done in this way to allow us to easily take it into a separate file as a plugin. But more on that later.

Applying the plugin to an existing schema

The next step is to pull these paths into our existing schemas. We can update our projectSchema and taskSchema definitions to remove the createdOn and createdBy paths. Instead, after each of the schemas are defined, we can link the creationInfo plugin to them as shown here:

```
projectSchema.plugin(creationInfo);
taskSchema.plugin(creationInfo);
```

That's all we need to do. If you run your application again, everything will still work as before, including any defaults and validators set, but your code has less repetition. The flipside of this is that your schemas are no longer self-contained and may be harder to read.

Using an external file

In order to make the code really re-usable and portable, we need to have it in an external file, not embedded in our db.js file. If we do this we can reference it from multiple files, and easily copy it to other projects. Create a new file called creationInfo.js in the model folder, with the following content:

```
var mongoose = require( 'mongoose' );
module.exports = exports = function creationInfo (schema, options) {
   schema.add({createdOn: { type: Date, default: Date.now }});
   schema.add({createdBy: { type: mongoose.Schema.Types.ObjectId, ref:
'User', required: true}});
};
```

Here we have required mongoose and just slightly modified our creationInfo function to become a module export function. In our db.js file, we can remove the creationInfo function and require our new file instead.

```
var creationInfo = require('./creationInfo');
```

And we're good to go! We've created a re-usable schema plugin—nice and easy. You can see how by doing this you can quickly build up a re-usable library of your own schema plugins.

Using schema middleware

Plugins also have access to all of the middleware available to schemas. There are two types of middleware hooks:

- `pre`: This middleware is for before the method has completed
- `post`: This is for after the method has completed

You can use these to hook into the methods `save` (which we'll look at in just a moment), `init`, `validate`, and `remove`.

Let's take a look at creating a schema plugin for the `modifiedOn` path that we have used in all of our schemas. What would be really great is if we can not only define the path in the plugin, but also set the value—this is where plugins and middleware meet perfectly.

Let's create a new file `model/modifiedOn.js` and require it in `model/db.js`, as shown in the following:

```
var modifiedOn = require('./modifiedOn');
```

In the new `model/modifiedOn.js` file, add the following code:

```
var mongoose = require( 'mongoose' );
module.exports = exports = function modifiedOn (schema, options) {
  schema.add({ modifiedOn: Date });

  schema.pre('save', function (next) {
    this.modifiedOn = Date.now();
    next();
  });
};
```

This will do two things, which are:

- Add the `modifiedOn` path with a SchemaType of `Date`
- Set the value to be the current date and time just before the document is saved

This removes the need to manually set the value each time we run an update operation on any of the schemas. So we can go through our code and remove the other instances of `user.modifiedOn = Date.now()`, `project.modifiedOn = Date.now()` and `thisTask.modifiedOn = Date.now()` as they are all handled in one place, every time any document (or subdocument) is saved. How's that for not repeating yourself?

The final step is to remove the `modifiedOn` definitions from each schema, and reference the plugin instead:

```
userSchema.plugin(modifiedOn);
projectSchema.plugin(modifiedOn);
taskSchema.plugin(modifiedOn);
```

Not just for plugins

This `schema.pre` middleware can also be used directly on the parent schema itself. We could quite easily have had this for example on an individual schema:

```
projectSchema.pre('save', function (next) {
  this.modifiedOn = Date.now();
  next();
});
```

Sharing with the community

Mongoose plugins are not just re-usable for you, you can share them with the rest of the community. By packaging them up as npm modules, and tagging them with "mongoose", they will become available in the Mongoose plugins directory.

There are already a large number of community-submitted plugins available that include adding support for a long number SchemaType, validation helpers, and authentication and user management plugins.

You can find the directory, and submission guidelines at the following link:

```
http://plugins.mongoosejs.com
```

Summary

In this chapter, we've seen how we can take repeated paths from our schemas and turn them into a single Mongoose plugin. We've learned how to create them as separate files, include them in our application, and also use schema middleware to set data on a save operation. We have used all of this knowledge to create plugins and add them to our MongoosePM application, tidying up our code and removing repetition.

This is the final chapter of *Mongoose for Application Development*. By now you should have the tools and understanding to enable you to build a web application based on everything Mongoose has to offer. I'm sure that by now you will agree that Mongoose is a very useful addition to the Node.js and MongoDB technology stack.

Index

Q

QueryBuilder interface
  about 68
  single-query operation, using 69, 70

R

remove() method 92
res.json() method 74
re-usable schema plugins
  about 117
  adding, to existing schema 118
  creating 117
  external file, using 118
  schema middleware, using 119
  sharing, with community 120
routes
  for project management 50
  for user management 50

S

schema, Mongoose
  __v 38
  about 14, 31
  code 44
  collection name, setting 42
  datatypes 32
  data, validating 37
  default value, setting 36, 37
  field sizes 32
  location, for writing 35
  models, building 40
  modifying 36
  Project schema, creating 39
  Project schema, improving 40
  userSchema 38
  writing 35
single project, finding
  findById, used 78
  route setup 78, 79
  view, creating 80
single-query operation
  using 69
single-threaded 8

single user, searching
  findOnes used 71
  homepage links, adding 73
  login action, creating 72, 73
  login form, creating 71
static helper methods
  about 70
  Model.findById(ObjectID) 70
  Model.findOne(query) 70
  Model.find(query) 70
string datatype, Mongoose schema 32
subdocuments
  about 110, 111
  creating 112
  deleting 114
  retrieving 113
  saving 112
  specific subdocument, accessing 113
  validating 112
Supervisor
  URL 60

T

technology stack
  Express 12
  MongoDB 11
  Node.js 8
technology stack, installation
  about 15
  Express.js, installing 17
  MongoDB, installing 16
  Mongoose, installing 17
  Node.js, installing 15
  npm, installing 15
  prerequisites 15

U

update() method 81, 84
user
  deleting 94
  editing 85
user creating
  confirmation page, displaying 63
  create project functionality, adding 64

Thank you for buying
Mongoose for Application Development

About Packt Publishing

Packt, pronounced 'packed', published its first book "*Mastering phpMyAdmin for Effective MySQL Management*" in April 2004 and subsequently continued to specialize in publishing highly focused books on specific technologies and solutions.

Our books and publications share the experiences of your fellow IT professionals in adapting and customizing today's systems, applications, and frameworks. Our solution based books give you the knowledge and power to customize the software and technologies you're using to get the job done. Packt books are more specific and less general than the IT books you have seen in the past. Our unique business model allows us to bring you more focused information, giving you more of what you need to know, and less of what you don't.

Packt is a modern, yet unique publishing company, which focuses on producing quality, cutting-edge books for communities of developers, administrators, and newbies alike. For more information, please visit our website: www.packtpub.com.

About Packt Open Source

In 2010, Packt launched two new brands, Packt Open Source and Packt Enterprise, in order to continue its focus on specialization. This book is part of the Packt Open Source brand, home to books published on software built around Open Source licences, and offering information to anybody from advanced developers to budding web designers. The Open Source brand also runs Packt's Open Source Royalty Scheme, by which Packt gives a royalty to each Open Source project about whose software a book is sold.

Writing for Packt

We welcome all inquiries from people who are interested in authoring. Book proposals should be sent to author@packtpub.com. If your book idea is still at an early stage and you would like to discuss it first before writing a formal book proposal, contact us; one of our commissioning editors will get in touch with you.

We're not just looking for published authors; if you have strong technical skills but no writing experience, our experienced editors can help you develop a writing career, or simply get some additional reward for your expertise.

Ext JS 4 Web Application Development Cookbook

ISBN: 978-1-84951-686-0   Paperback: 488 pages

Over 110 easy-to-follow recipes backed up with real-life examples, walking you through basic Ext JS features to advanced application design using Sencha's Ext JS

1. Learn how to build Rich Internet Applications with the latest version of the Ext JS framework in a cookbook style

2. From creating forms to theming your interface, you will learn the building blocks for developing the perfect web application

3. Easy to follow recipes step through practical and detailed examples which are all fully backed up with code, illustrations, and tips

OGRE 3D 1.7 Application Development Cookbook

ISBN: 978-1-84951-456-9   Paperback: 306 pages

Over 50 recipes to provide world-class 3D graphicssolutions with OGRE 3D

1. Dive into the advanced features of OGRE 3D such as scene querying and visibility analysis

2. Give stunning effects to your application through suitable use of lights, special effects, and views

3. Surf through the full spectrum of OGRE 3D animation methods and insert flashy multimedia

Please check **www.PacktPub.com** for information on our titles

web2py Application Development Cookbook

ISBN: 978-1-84951-546-7   Paperback: 364 pages

Over 110 recipes to master this full-stack Python web framework

1. Take your web2py skills to the next level by dipping into delicious, usable recipes in this cookbook

2. Learn advanced web2py usage from building advanced forms to creating PDF reports

3. Written by developers of the web2py project with plenty of code examples for interesting and comprehensive learning

CouchDB and PHP Web Development Beginner's Guide

ISBN: 978-1-84951-358-6   Paperback: 304 pages

Get your PHP application from conception to deployment by leveraging CouchDB's robust features

1. Build and deploy a flexible Social Networking application using PHP and leveraging key features of CouchDB to do the heavy lifting

2. Explore the features and functionality of CouchDB, by taking a deep look into Documents, Views, Replication, and much more.

3. Conceptualize a lightweight PHP framework from scratch and write code that can easily port to other frameworks

Please check **www.PacktPub.com** for information on our titles

Printed in Great Britain
by Amazon.co.uk, Ltd.,
Marston Gate.